Torahdike English

The Young Ben Torah's Guide to Learning English

Learning to spell

When learning to spell words, it is useful to have a strategy in place for how to learn. The following 7-step process is useful as a system to aid you in learning to spell the words you learn.

Step 1 LOOK at the word. Notice the letters, pay attention to their sounds, and observe any distinct patterns or formations.

Step 2 SAY the word. Make sure to pronounce it correctly and pay attention to the sounds that the letters make.

Step 3 SPELL the word aloud. Recite each letter distinctly with your mouth as you pay attention to what you speak with your ears. Engaging each of your senses helps you remember.

Step 4 COPY the word. As you write each letter, first look at it as it is printed and pay attention to its appearance and sound, then write it out on your paper.

Step 5 PICTURE the word in your mind. Using your mind's eye, imagine the entire word spelled before you. Focus on each letter as it appears in your mind's eye, its appearance and its sound, together with the entire word's appearance and sound,,

Step 6 Cover the word and WRITE it. Writing the word from memory forces the short-term recall area of your brain to quickly review and remember the way the word is spelled. Writing it out gives you a means of checking how well you actually remember, and helps cement what you just reviewed.

Step 7 CHECK for accuracy. Compare the word you wrote from memory to the correctly printed word in front of you. Notice any inaccuracies. If there was a mistake, repeat steps 1-6.

This work should be done for the words in each lesson to learn the spelling of the words. This is in addition to the exercises and classwork that you will be assigned each week to help you review the meanings and usages of the words.

Spelling Lesson 1

Key Concepts
- base word
- suffix
- related forms of words
- parts of speech (noun, verb, adjective, adverb)

A **base word** is a word before any changes have been made.

A **suffix** is a word ending that changes the use of a word or its function.

Words that share the same base word, but have different prefixes or suffixes are **related forms** of the base word.

Related forms of the same base word may be different **parts of speech**. They may be nouns, adjectives, verbs, or adverbs.

There are four parts of speech used to categorize most of the spelling words in this book. **Nouns** (n.) are persons, places, or things (both things you can touch like objects, and things you cannot touch like ideas). One example of a noun is <u>apple</u>. **Adjectives** (adj.) are words that are used to modify (describe, limit, or tell you about) nouns. For example, a <u>red</u> apple. **Verbs** (v.) are actions (like eating or jumping) or states of being (like awake, alive, existing). **Adverbs** (adv.) are words that modify (describe, limit, or tell you about) verbs. For example, eating the apple <u>quickly</u>.

Lesson 1 Spelling Rule: When you add a suffix that begins with a vowel to a word that ends with silent e, drop the final e.

Suffixes used in this lesson, together with their meanings:
- -ant (that has or shows)
- -ance (act of, state of being)
- -al (of, like, act of)
- -ion (the act of, condition of, or result of)
- -ure (act or result of being, a thing or group that)
- -ial (of, like, act of)
- -ing (the action of)
- -ive (of, having the nature of)

1. PLEASE + ANT = PLEASANT
2. RESEMBLE + ANCE = RESEMBLANCE
3. PROPOSE + AL = PROPOSAL
4. PRACTICE + AL = PRACTICAL
5. IGNITE + ION = IGNITION
6. ENCLOSE + URE = ENCLOSURE
7. FINANCE + IAL = FINANCIAL
8. RESCUE + ING = RESCUING
9. RAISE + ING = RAISING
10. RELATE + IVE = RELATIVE
11. OBSERVE + ANT = OBSERVANT
12. GUIDE + ANCE = GUIDANCE
13. REHEARSE + AL = REHEARSAL
14. GLOBE + AL = GLOBAL
15. INDICATE + ION = INDICATION
16. LEGISLATE + URE = LEGISLATURE
17. RACE + IAL = RACIAL
18. ARGUE + ING = ARGUING
19. WRITE + ING = WRITING
20. COOPERATE + IVE = COOPERATIVE

Pay attention to the spelling words.

1. What eight different suffixes have been added to form spelling words? _____ _____ _____

   _____ _____ _____ _____ _____

2. Does each suffix begin with a consonant or a vowel? _____

3. Before the suffix is added, each word ends with a letter that is not pronounced. What is that

   final silent letter? _____

4. What happens to the final silent letter when the suffix is added?

   _____

When you add a suffix that begins with a vowel to a word that ends with silent **e**, drop the final **e**.

Spelling Dictionary

1. **ar·gue** — *v.* **–gued, –gue·ing**[1] to give reasons, to dispute, to show
2. **ar·gu·ing** — *v.* giving reasons, quarreling
3. **co·op·e·rate, co-op·e·rate**[2] — *v.* **–rat·ed, –rat·ing** to work together
4. **co·op·er·a·tive** — *adj.* Cooperating or willing to cooperate
5. **en·close** — *v.* **–closed, –clos·ing** to shut in or surround, to insert or hold in an envelope
6. **en·clo·sure** — *n.* an act of enclosing, being enclosed, something that encloses
7. **fi·nance** — *n.* the conduct of money matters   *–v.*[3] **–nanced, –nancing** to supply money, to manage money
8. **fi·nan·cial** — *adj.* of finance
9. **glo·bal** — *adj.* worldwide
10. **globe** — *n.* the planet earth; a spherical shape
11. **gui·dance** — *n.* an act of guiding, a thing that guides
12. **guide** — *v.* **–guid·ed, –guid·ing** to assist, advise, or supervise   *–n.* a person or thing that guides
13. **ig·nite** — *v.* **–ni·ted, –ni·ting** to set or catch on fire
14. **ig·ni·tion** — *n.* act of or means of igniting
15. **in·di·cate** — *v.* **–cat·ed, –cat·ing** point, demonstrate
16. **in·di·ca·tion** — *n.* something that indicates or shows
17. **leg·is·late** — *v.* **–lat·ed, –lat·ing** to enact laws
18. **leg·is·la·ture** — *n.* a body of persons with the power to make laws
19. **ob·serv·ant** — *adj.* paying careful attention, alert, perceptive
20. **ob·serve** — *v.* **–served, –serv·ing** to see, pay attention, obey, remark
21. **plea·sant** — *adj.* giving satisfaction or delight; agreeable
22. **please** — *v.* **pleased, plea·sing** to give satisfaction or delight
23. **plea·sing** — *adj.* giving pleasure and satisfaction; pleasant or agreeable to the senses [the *pleasing* sound of music]
24. **prac·ti·cal** — *adj.* usable, workable, useful, sensible
25. **pra·tice** — *v.* **–ticed, –ti·cing** habit, custom, action
26. **pro·po·sal** — *n.* a plan or action proposed
27. **pro·pose** — *v.* **–posed, –pos·sing** suggest
28. **race** — *n.* a group of people sharing descent, or traits
29. **ra·cial** — *adj.* of a race, between races
30. **raise** — *v.* **raised, rai·sing** to lift, to increase in force, to cause to grow
31. **rais·ing** — *n.* an act of lifting or causing to grow   *–v.* lifting, causing to grow
32. **re·hearsal** — *n.* a practice performance of a show

---

1   The dictionary will usually list related forms after the entry word. Sometimes, if the related word is significantly different from the base word it gets a separate entry. In the first few lessons, most of the related words also were listed as separate entries. Often, the dictionary abbreviates the related words and begins with the syllable that is different from the entry word. The missing first part of the word is represented by the hyphen.

2   When there is another way to spell a word, it is called a variant, and is often listed after the entry word. More on variants in Lesson 17.

3   The definitions are given for each word under the same entry, separated by the part of speech that it is used. The related words are listed between the part of speech and the definitions.

33. **re·hearse** — *v.* **–hearsed, – hear·sing** to practice a performance
34. **re·late** — *v.* **–la·ted, –la·ting** to tell, to cause or have an association
    with
35. **re·la·tive** — *adj.* being family with each other — *n.* a member
    of the family
36. **res·cue** — *v.* **–cued, –cu·ing** save
37. **res·cu·ing** — *n.* an act of saving — *v.* saving
38. **re·sem·blance** — *n.* degree of likeness, sort of likeness
39. **re·sem·ble** — *v.* **–bled, -bling** to be like or similar to
40. **write** — *v.* **wri·ting** to compose characters on a surface, to express
    ideas in script
41. **wri·ting** — *n.* something written — *v.* forming characters,
    expressing ideas in script

Practicing the words
Writing
A. Answer each question with a complete sentence that uses a related form of the spelling word in the sentence by adding a suffix to the underlined word.

1. Does Herb resemble his brother? _____

_____

2. Has the cast begun to rehearse the play? _____

_____

3. Did everyone on the team cooperate? _____

_____

4. Is the person you phoned related to you? _____

_____

5. Did Lana propose her idea at the last meeting? _____

_____

6. Are you going to raise corn in your garden? _____

_____

7. What is the name of a holiday that your family will observe this month? _____

_____

8. Did yesterday's weather please you? _____

_____

9. What practice does Rabbi Menasche encourage everyone to do? _____

_____

10. Who is going to ignite the first firework of the display? _____

_____

11. What is the next project that Mr. Reichman will finance? _____

_____

12. Whose pet is Tzirel about to <u>rescue</u> from the wind storm? _____

_____

13. Who will <u>guide</u> the boys as they prepare for the Shabbaton? _____

_____

14. What is causing changes in weather around the <u>globe</u>? _____

_____

15. How does a driver <u>indicate</u> in which direction he will turn? _____

_____

16. How did the zookeepers <u>enclose</u> the new group of monkeys? _____

_____

17. What new law did Congress <u>legislate</u> recently? _____

_____

18. What is your opinion with regards to discriminating against people of a different <u>race</u>?

_____

19. What is the name of someone who chose to <u>argue</u> with Korach against Moshe Rabbeinu?

_____

20. To whom will you <u>write</u> about the damaged item you received?

_____

B.   A **base word** is a word before any changes have been made. A **suffix** can be added to a base word to change the way it is used.

Does the weather <u>please</u> you? (*please* is a verb)

Yes, the weather is very <u>pleasing</u> today. (*pleasing* is an adjective)

The weather has been <u>pleasant</u> for several days. (*pleasant* is an adjective)

The underlined words are **related forms** of the base word **please**. Related forms of the same base word may be different parts of speech. They may be nouns, verbs, adjectives, or adverbs. Write the base form of each word and the abbreviation of which part of speech it is[4]. Then add the suffix to the base form and write the related form, along with the abreviation of which part of speech it is. Remember to drop the final silent **e** of the base form.

	Base Form		Related Form
1. pleasing		+ ant	
2. resembling		+ ance	
3. financed		+ ial	
4. legislating		+ ure	
5. guiding		+ ance	
6. writer		+ ing	
7. argued		+ ing	
8. practicing		+ al	
9. proposing		+ al	
10. ignited		+ ion	
11. enclosing		+ ure	
12. rescued		+ ing	
13. raised		+ ing	
14. relation		+ ive	
15. observing		+ ant	
16. rehearsed		+ al	
17. globes		+ al	
18. indicated		+ ion	
19. races		+ ial	
20. cooperation		+ ive	

---

4   If there is more than one possibility, pick the first that is listed in the dictionary.

12

C. Proofreading

Cross out the misspelled words in the following paragraphs. Then rewrite them, correctly spelled on the spaces below.

I was unpleasantly surprised last week when I bumped into an old classmate of mine from elementary school. His behavior bore no resembleance to the way I remembered him as my old friend. He used to be a pleaseant, well-mannered boy who liked to help out others. But now he seems to be a very different person. He is now a politician and a member of our state's lejislacher. He told me about his proposel to enact a new law that prevents collectors from soliciting donations in synagogues. He no longer wants to see them disturb people who try to pray while they are raiseing money to help themselves out of their finantial difficulties. His new law would require all rellatives of anyone who is poor to be cooperativ in rescyuing them from their circumstances. I tried argyueing with him that this is not practickal for most people and would deprive observent Jews from fulfilling the mitzvah of charity. I am disturbed at the possibility of such an outcome. When I sought advice, I received guidence to try igniteing the outrage of the globel community, to encourage them to try riting to the lawmakers to prevent this from happening.

1. _____

2. _____

3. _____

4. _____

5. _____

6. _____

7. _____

8. _____

9. _____

10. _____

11. _____

12. _____

13. _____

14. _____

15. _____

16. _____

13

D. Fill in the following sentences with the appropriate spelling words.

1. That __ __ __ __ __ __ __ __ __ is intended for the animal exhibit.

2. Bird watchers are generally __ __ __ __ __ __ __ __ __ people.

3. The state __ __ __ __ __ __ __ __ __ __ __ is now in session with the required number of members.

4. I noticed the __ __ __ __ __ __ __ __ __ __ __ between the two brothers.

5. The accountant gave the new store owner __ __ __ __ __ __ __ __ __ advice.

6. Our school has a number of __ __ __ __ __ __ __ __ counselors.

7. A __ __ __ __ __ __ __ __ breeze blew along the front porch.

8. My family is proud of our __ __ __ __ __ __ heritage.

9. The senate will vote on the __ __ __ __ __ __ __ __ in the near future.

10. The firefighter received a medal for __ __ __ __ __ __ __ __ __ the trapped child.

11. Zalman made sure to attend every __ __ __ __ __ __ __ __ __ __ of the choir.

12. There is never to be any __ __ __ __ __ __ __ with a teacher.

13. We seek a __ __ __ __ __ __ __ __ __ __ solution to the problem?

14. The walkathon is __ __ __ __ __ __ __ money for a worthy cause.

15. Satellites enable __ __ __ __ __ __ communication.

16. In this class you will be __ __ __ __ __ __ __ some essays.

17. The driver attempted to insert the wrong key in the __ __ __ __ __ __ __ __.

18. The director of the play is a __ __ __ __ __ __ __ __ __ of hers.

19. Turn on your blinkers to provide __ __ __ __ __ __ __ __ __ __ of your intention to turn.

20. Cleaning up the neighborhood was a __ __ __ __ __ __ __ __ __ __ __ __ effort.

Key Concepts
- base word
- suffix
- related forms of words
- parts of speech (noun, verb, adjective, adverb)

A **base word** is a word before any changes have been made.

A **suffix** is a word ending that changes the use of a word or its function.

Words that share the same base word, but have different prefixes or suffixes are **related forms** of the base word.

Related forms of the same base word may be different **parts of speech**. They may be nouns, adjectives, verbs, or adverbs.

There are four parts of speech used to categorize most of the spelling words in this book. **Nouns** (n.) are persons, places, or things (both things you can touch like objects, and things you cannot touch like ideas). **Adjectives** (adj.) are words that are used to modify (describe, limit, or tell you about) nouns. **Verbs** (v.) are actions (like eating or jumping) or states of being (like awake, alive, existing). **Adverbs** (adv.) are words that modify (describe, limit, or tell you about) verbs.

Remember the old rule: **I** before **e** except after **c**; or when sounding a, as in n<u>eigh</u>bor or w<u>eigh</u>.

Lesson 2 Spelling Rule: When you add a suffix that begins with a consonant to a word that ends with silent e, keep the final e.

Suffixes used in this lesson, together with their meanings:
- -ity (forms a noun from an adjective; having the quality of; being in the state or condition)
- -ly (forms an adjective from a noun, or adverb from adjective; like, characteristic of, in a specified manner)
- -ing (indicates present tense of verb; forms noun from a verb)
- -ive (of; having the nature of)
- -less (without; that cannot; that does not)
- -ment (forms a noun from a verb; a result, the act or process; the state or fact)
- -ion (act, condition, or result of)
- -ory (having the function or effect of, pertaining to)

1. FESTIVE	+ ITY	= FESTIVITY	+ LY	= FESTIVELY
2. SEVERE	+ ITY	= SEVERITY	+ LY	= SEVERELY
3. TIME	+ ING	= TIMING	+ LY	= TIMELY
4. LOVE	+ ING	= LOVING	+ LY	= LOVELY
5. LIKE	+ ING	= LIKING	+ LY	= LIKELY
6. COMPLETE	+ ING	= COMPLETING	+ LY	= COMPLETELY
7. DEFINITE	+ ION	= DEFINITION	+ LY	= DEFINITELY
8. INTENSE	+ IVE	= INTENSIVE	+ LY	= INTENSELY
9. DEFENSE	+ IVE	= DEFENSIVE	+ LESS	= DEFENSELESS
10. PRICE	+ ING	= PRICING	+ LESS	= PRICELESS
11. BLAME	+ ING	= BLAMING	+ LESS	= BLAMELESS
12. AGE	+ ING	= AGING	+ LESS	= AGELESS
13. SENSE	+ ORY	= SENSORY	+ LESS	= SENSELESS
14. CONFINE	+ ING	= CONFINING	+ MENT	= CONFINEMENT
15. ENDORSE	+ ING	= ENDORSING	+ MENT	= ENDORSEMENT
16. MEASURE	+ ING	= MEASURING	+ MENT	= MEASUREMENT
17. AMUSE	+ ING	= AMUSING	+ MENT	= AMUSEMENT
18. ENGAGE	+ ING	= ENGAGING	+ MENT	= ENGAGEMENT
19. STATE	+ ING	= STATING	+ MENT	= STATEMENT
20. ACHIEVE	+ ING	= ACHIEVING	+ MENT	= ACHIEVEMENT

Pay attention to the spelling words.
1. Why is the final silent e dropped from the words in the first column to form the word in the

   middle column? _____

2. _____
3. What three suffixes have been added to form the words in the last column?

   _____ _____ _____
4. Does each suffix begin with a consonant or a vowel? _____
5. What happens to the final e when a suffix beginning with a consonant is added?

   _____

When you add a suffix that begins with a consonant to a word that ends with silent **e**, keep the final **e**. When you add a suffix that begins with a vowel to a word that ends with silent **e**, drop the final **e**.

1. **a·chieve** — *v.* **a·chieved, a·chiev·ing** to succeed in doing; to accomplish
2. **a·chieve·ment** — *n.* success; an achievement or thing achieved
3. **a·chiev·ing** — *v.* present tense of achieve
4. **age** — *n.* the time that a person or thing existed since birth or beginning — *v.* **aged, ag·ing** or **age·ing**[5] to grow old or become mature
5. **age·less** — *adj.* seemingly not growing older; eternal
6. **age·ing** — *v.* present tense of age
7. **a·muse** — *v.* **a·mused, a·mus·ing** entertain; keep pleasantly interested
8. **a·muse·ment** — *n.* the condition of being amused; something that amuses
9. **a·mus·ing** — *v.* present tense of amuse
10. **blame** — *v.* **blamed, blam·ing** to find fault with; criticize
11. **blame·less** — *adj.* not deserving to be blamed
12. **blam·ing** — *v.* present tense of blame
13. **com·plete** — *adj.* entire; whole; lacking no part — *v.* **–plet·ed, –plet·ing** to end; finish
14. **com·plete·ly** — *adv.* in a complete manner
15. **com·plet·ing** — *v.* present tense of complete
16. **con·fine** — *n.* border — *v.* **–fined , –fin·ing** to enclose; to keep shut in
17. **con·fine·ment** — *n.* a confining or being confined
18. **con·fin·ing** — *v.* present tense of confine
19. **de·fense** — *n.* protection; support
20. **de·fense·less** — *adj.* lacking defense; helpless
21. **de·fen·sive** — *adj.* feeling under attack ane needing to justify
22. **def·i·nite** — *adj.* precise and clear in meaning; certain; positive
23. **def·i·nite·ly** — *adj.* in a definite manner
24. **def·i·ni·tion** — *n.* statement of the meaning of a word or phrase
25. **en·dorse** — *v.* **–dorsed, –dors·ing** to support; to give approval
26. **en·dorse·ment** — *n.* a statement endorsing someone or thing
27. **en·dors·ing** — *v.* present tense of endorse
28. **en·gage** — *v.* **–gaged, –gag·ing** to occupy the attention of; hire; to bind by promise; to betroth
29. **en·gage·ment** — *n.* a betrothal; an appointment to meet someone or go somewhere
30. **en·gag·ing** — *v.* present tense of engage; — *adj.* attractive, charming
31. **fes·tive** — *adj.* of or for a feast or festival; joyous, merry
32. **fes·tive·ly** — *adv.* in a manner relating to a feast or festival
33. **fes·tiv·i·ty** — *n.* merrymaking, gaiety
34. **in·tense** — *adj.* occurring in a high degree; very strong
35. **in·tense·ly** — *adv.* in an intense manner
36. **in·ten·sive** — *adj.* characterized by intensity; thorough
37. **like** — *n.* preference — *v.* **liked, lik·ing** want; wish; take pleasure in
38. **like·ly** — *adj.* reasonably expected; suitable; having good prospects — *adv.* probably
39. **lik·ing** — *n.* preference; taste; pleasure
40. **love** — *n.* warm feelings — *v.* **loved, lov·ing** to feel or show love

---

5   This is a variant spelling of the word. More on that in Lesson 17

41. **love·ly**   *adj.* having qualities that inspire love
42. **lov·ing**   *adj.* feeling or showing love
43. **mea·sure**   *n.* the extent or dimensions of anything   *–v.* **–sured,**
   –sur·ing to find out or estimate the measure
44. **mea·sure·ment**   *n.* a measuring or being measured; the quantity or extent determined by
   measuring
45. **mea·sur·ing**   *v.* present tense of measure
46. **price**   *n.* amount of money asked or paid for something   *–v.* **priced,**
   pric·ing to set a price
47. **price·less**   *adj.* too valuable to be measured by price
48. **pri·cing**   *v.* present tense of price
49. **sense**   *n.* feeling; perception; understanding   *–v.* **sensed, sens·ing** to
   perceive or understand
50. **sense·less**   *adj.* not showing good sense; foolish
51. **sen·so·ry**   *adj.* of the senses or sensation
52. **se·vere**   *adj.* harsh or strict; intense; difficult
53. **se·vere·ly**   *adv.* in a harsh or strict manner
54. **se·ver·i·ty**   *n.* strictness, harshness, extreme hardship
55. **state**   *n.* set of circumstances; condition   *–v.* **sta·ted, sta·ting** to set or
   establish by specifying
56. **state·ment**   *n.* the act of stating or the thing stated
57. **stat·ing**   *v.* present tense of state
58. **time**   *n.* occurrence, duration   *–v.* **timed, tim·ing** to measure duration
59. **time·ly**   *adj.* happening at a suitable time
60. **tim·ing**   *n.* arranging the time of something so as to get the best results
   –v. present tense of time

Practicing the words

A. Write the base form of each word and its abbreviated part of speech[6]. Then write the related form made by adding **ing** to the base and write its abbreviated part of speech.

		Base Form	**ing** Form
1	achievement	_____	_____
2	ageless	_____	_____
3	completely	_____	_____
4	confinement	_____	_____
5	timely	_____	_____
6	amusement	_____	_____
7	engagement	_____	_____
8	blameless	_____	_____
9	measurement	_____	_____
10	endorsement	_____	_____

---

6   If the word can be used as more than one part of speech, write the first one listed in the dictionary.

B. Proofreading
Cross out the misspelled words in these announcements. Write the words correctly

ENTERTAINMENT THIS MONTH

Here for a limited engagment!
SuperMalach 4
A marvelous achievemint in moviemaking!
Definitely one movie to see!

Add to your holiday festivety
with **Family Day** at exciting
Westernland Amusment Park.
All children free!
(You'll never read another statment like this!)

Super Circus!
Come see it all!
Vicious lions (in safe confinment)!
Death-defying acts of untold severety!
Comic clowns and amusing animals!
Music, costumes, and other sensery delights!

Super Sidewalk Sale
All merchants (by definiteon) will have
their merchandise out on the sidewalks!
All priceing will be unbelievably low,
Come and browse!

Miracle Health Club Picnic·
Defenseve about your weight?
If your measurments don't change after an
intenseve day with us, we'll give you a
year's membership free!
*Paid endorsment.

1. _____

2. _____

3. _____

4. _____

5. _____

6. _____

7. _____

8. _____

9. _____

10. _____

11. _____

12. _____

13. _____

14. _____

Writing

C. Answer each question with a complete sentence that uses a related form of the spelling word in the sentence by adding a suffix to the underlined word.

1. What is a <u>festive</u> custom that your famiy will do this month? _____

_____

2. What is the meaning of the <u>severe</u> expression on the principal's face today? _____

_____

3. What <u>time</u> will Yizkor be recited on Yom Kippur? _____

_____

4. Which part of Sukkos do you <u>love</u> most? _____

_____

5. Which of the Baalei Tefillah do you <u>like</u> best? _____

_____

6. How much do you expect to pay for a <u>complete</u> set of Arba Minim? _____

_____

7. Did Agudas Yisroel take a <u>definite</u> stance about the school vouchers? _____

_____

8. What part of Yom Kippur tefillos do you find very <u>intense</u>? _____

_____

9. What <u>defense</u> will you use to protect against bees or wasps in your sukkah? _____

_____

10. What determines the <u>price</u> of a chinuch set of Arba Minim? _____

_____

11. Who is to <u>blame</u> for the disruption during the tekiyos? _____

_____

21

12. Until what <u>age</u> do children eat on Yom Kippur? _____

_____

13. What is the <u>sense</u> of spending so much time praying if one does not understand the meaning of

his words? _____

_____

14. Why did Shmuel <u>confine</u> his rabbit to his backyard? _____

_____

15. Why did the Vaad <u>endorse</u> the Democratic candidate for town council? _____

_____

16. Do you know if it is permitted to <u>measure</u> a shofar on Rosh Hashanah? _____

_____

17. Does any portion of Yomim Noraim preparations <u>amuse</u> you? _____

_____

18. What precautions will you take not to <u>engage</u> in idle speech? _____

_____

19. What is the <u>state</u> of the shul's financial circumstances? _____

_____

20. What goals do you wish to <u>achieve</u> during this coming school year? _____

_____

D. Proofreading

The right base word used with the incorrect suffix or ending can make a confusing story. Mrs. Mixit has botched up her narrative paragraph[7]. Find the ten mismatched words in her story. Then write the spelling words that could be used to replace them.

The accidental loss of the pricely ring seemed sensory. Measurement the value of the loving antique, which had been given to my great-grandmother for her engaging, was impossible. It was definition a possession that was not liking to be replaced. Our intensely search finally uncovered the culprit. He was swinging on his perch, looking completing blaming, with the ring in his beak!

1. _____

2. _____

3. _____

4. _____

5. _____

6. _____

7. _____

8. _____

9. _____

10. _____

---

7   A narrative paragraph is one that tells a story.

E. Fill in the following sentences with the appropriate spelling words.

1. The first night of סליחות, the בית מדרש was __ __ __ __ __ __ __ __ __ __ full of people.

2. No one is __ __ __ __ __ __ __ you for the mistake.

3. On Shabbos, __ __ __ __ __ __ __ __ __ __ __ (מדידה) is only permitted for a מצוה purpose.

4. Over the year, you will be __ __ __ __ __ __ __ __ __ great results.

5. The holiday season is a time of __ __ __ __ __ __ __ __ __.

6. The superstorm __ __ __ __ __ __ __ __ damaged the fruit trees.

7. The package will __ __ __ __ __ __ __ __ __ __ arrive by Thursday.

8. The cheese was wrapped up and stored for __ __ __ __ __.

9. What sort of __ __ __ __ __ __ __ __ __ park would only have four roller coasters?

10. A comedian needs good __ __ __ __ __ __ to be funny.

11. The soldiers underwent __ __ __ __ __ __ __ __ __ training.

12. This __ __ __ __ __ __ __ __ __ argument should stop immediately.

13. Mendel was looking forward to celebrating his sister's __ __ __ __ __ __ __ __ __ __ __.

14. The weather had been unusually __ __ __ __ __ __ for autumn.

15. The young fawn was __ __ __ __ __ __ __ __ __ __ __ without its mother.

16. Do you find the rules __ __ __ __ __ __ __ __ __?

17. The agency wrote a letter __ __ __ __ __ __ __ the options.

18. If you study dilligently you are __ __ __ __ __ __ to get a good grade.

19. We are __ __ __ __ __ __ __ the tickets below last year's costs.

20. The candidate's __ __ __ __ __ __ __ __ __ __ __ made him a popular choice.

Spelling Lesson 3

Key Concepts
- base word
- suffix
- related forms of words
- parts of speech (noun, verb, adjective, adverb)
- hard and soft sounds
- possessive form of nouns

A **base word** is a word before any changes have been made.

A **suffix** is a word ending that changes the use of a word or its function.

Words that share the same base word, but have different prefixes or suffixes are **related forms** of the base word.

Related forms of the same base word may be different **parts of speech**. They may be nouns, adjectives, verbs, or adverbs.

There are four parts of speech used to categorize most of the spelling words in this book. **Nouns** (n.) are persons, places, or things (both things you can touch like objects, and things you cannot touch like ideas). **Adjectives** (adj.) are words that are used to modify (describe, limit, or tell you about) nouns. **Verbs** (v.) are actions (like eating or jumping) or states of being (like awake, alive, existing). **Adverbs** (adv.) are words that modify (describe, limit, or tell you about) verbs.

A hard sound is one that is short and explosive, that comes out of the mouth with a popping sound. It cannot be lengthened for an appreciable amount of time. Some examples of hard sounds are **b**, **p**, and **d**.

A soft sound is one that comes out of the mouth along with air in a sort of hissing sound. It can be short or lengthened without changing its sound. Some examples of soft sounds are **ch**, **s**, and **th**.

The **possessive** form of the noun shows that something belongs to a noun. The usual way to make a possessive form is to add **'s** to the noun (girl+**'s** = girl's, men+**'s** = men's).[8]

Remember: A word that describes an action is a verb: **decorate**.
　　　　　　 A word that names something is a noun: **decoration.**
　　　　　　　　 ate is a verb ending　 **ion** is a noun ending

Remember: The spelling rule from Lesson 1 was when you add a suffix that begins with a vowel to a word that ends with silent **e**, drop the final **e**.

The word ending pronounced **shun** is usually spelled **tion**. Many verbs that end with **ate** can be changed to nouns by adding the suffix **ion**. The hard **t** in **ate** becomes a soft **t** in **tion**.

　　　Suffixes used in this lesson, together with their meanings:
- -ate (indicating a verb)
- -ion (the act of, condition of, or result of)

---

8   See more about possessives in Lesson 14.

1. EQUATE	+	ION	=	EQUATION
2. SEPARATE	+	ION	=	SEPARATION
3. NARRATE	+	ION	=	NARRATION
4. DECORATE	+	ION	=	DECORATION
5. HIBERNATE	+	ION	=	HIBERNATION
6. LEGISLATE	+	ION	=	LEGISLATION
7. INFLATE	+	ION	=	INFLATION
8. IRRITATE	+	ION	=	IRRITATION
9. OBLIGATE	+	ION	=	OBLIGATION
10. CONGREGATE	+	ION	=	CONGREGATION
11. EVALUATE	+	ION	=	EVALUATION
12. CREATE	+	ION	=	CREATION
13. NAVIGATE	+	ION	=	NAVIGATION
14. COORDINATE	+	ION	=	COORDINATION
15. EVACUATE	+	ION	=	EVACUATION
16. GENERATE	+	ION	=	GENERATION
17. MANIPULATE	+	ION	=	MANIPULATION
18. DOMINATE	+	ION	=	DOMINATION
19. PARTICIPATE	+	ION	=	PARTICIPATION
20. ISOLATE	+	ION	=	ISOLATION

Pay attention to the spelling words.
All of the base words on this list end with the same three letters.

1. What are those letters? _____

2. Is the final **e** pronounced or silent? _____

3. Does the letter **t** have a hard sound (ra<u>t</u>e) or a soft sound (na<u>t</u>ion)? _____

4. What are the last four letters of each word after the ion suffix is added? _____

5. What happens to the final silent e? _____

6. Does the letter t have a hard or soft sound? _____

The word ending pronounced **shun** is usually spelled **tion**. Many verbs that end with **ate** can be changed to nouns by adding the suffix **ion**. The hard **t** in **ate** becomes a soft **t** in **tion**. It might help you to remember that the noun ending ends in **n** (io<u>n</u>).

Spelling Dictionary

1. **con·gre·gate**   *v.* **–ga·ted, –ga·ting** to come together, usually for a purpose
2. **con·gre·ga·tion**   *n.* 1. a gathering of people or things   2. a group of people meeting for religious worship
3. **co·or·di·nate, co-or·di·nate**[9]   *adj.* of equal order, rank, or importance [the *coordinate* main clauses in a compound sentence]   *–v.* **–na·ted, –na·ting** to bring into proper order or relation
4. **co·or·di·na·tion, co-or·di·na·tion**   *n.* 1. a bringing into proper order; adjusting   2. harmonious or coordinated action, as of muscles
5. **co·or·di·na·tor, co-or·di·na·tor**   *n.* one who coordinates
6. **cre·ate**   *v.* **–a·ted, –a·ting** to make or cause to come into being, to bring into existence through artistic means
7. **cre·a·tion**   *n.* anything created; esp., something original created by the imagination
8. **cre·a·tor**   *n.* one who creates
9. **dec·o·rate**   *v.* **–ra·ted, –ra·ting** 1. to make more attractive by adding ornament, color, etc.   2. to award a mark of honor
10. **dec·o·ra·tion**   *n.* 1. the act of decorating   2. anything used for decorating 3. a medal, badge, or similar token of honor
11. **dec·o·ra·tor**   *n.* one who decorates
12. **dom·i·nate**   *v.* **–na·ted, –na·ting** to rule or control by superior power or influence
13. **dom·i·na·tion**   *n.* 1. social control by dominating   2. power to dominate or defeat
14. **e·quate**   *v.* **–qua·ted, –qua·ting** 1. to consider as similar or the same   2. to be equivalent or parallel, as in mathematics   3. to make the same
15. **e·qua·tion**   *n.* a statement of equality between two entities, as shown by the equal sign (=) [a quadratic *equation*]
16. **e·vac·u·ate**   *v.* **–a·ted, –a·ting** to remove (inhabitants, troops, etc.) from (a place or area), as for protective purposes
17. **e·vac·u·a·tion**   *n.* 1. the act of removing the contents of something   2. the act of evacuating; leaving a place in an ordinary fasion
18. **e·val·u·ate**   *v.* **–a·ted, –a·ting** to judge or determine the worth or quality of; appraise
19. **e·val·u·a·tion**   *n.* 1. act of determining the worth of   2. an appraisal of the value of something
20. **gen·er·ate**   *v.* **–ra·ted, –ra·ting** 1. bring into existence; produce   2. make (offspring) by reproduction
21. **gen·er·a·tion**   *n.* 1. a single stage in the history of a family [father and daughter are two *generations*]   2. the average period (about thirty years) between the birth of one generation and the birth of the next
22. **gen·e·ra·tor**   *n.* one who or that generates

---

9   Variant means an alternate. When a word can be spelled in more than one way, the variant spelling is listed after the first (or main) entry word. The dictionary is showing that the word can be spelled with or without a hyphen. More on variants in Lesson 17.

23. **hi·ber·nate**   *v.* **–na·ted, –na·ting** to spend the winter in a dormant or inactive state

24. **hi·ber·na·tion**   *n. 1.* the dormant or resting state in which some animals pass the winter   2. the act of retiring into inactivity

25. **in·flate**   *v.* **–fla·ted, –fla·ting** 1. to exaggerate or make bigger   2. to fill with gas or air 3. to cause prices to rise by increasing the available currency or credit

26. **in·fla·tion**   *n. 1.* the act of filling something with air   2. an increase in the amount of money in circulation that causes a fall in its value and a rise in prices

27. **ir·ri·tate**   *v.* **–ta·ted, –ta·ting** cause annoyance in; disturb, especially by minor irritations

28. **ir·ri·ta·tion**   *n. 1.* the act or condition of being irritated   2. a sore or inflamed condition

29. **i·so·late**   *v.* **–la·ted, –la·ting** place or set apart; separate

30. **i·so·la·tion**   *n.* a setting apart or being set apart from others

31. **leg·is·late**   *v.* **–la·ted, –la·ting** to make laws

32. **leg·is·la·tion**   *n. 1.* the making of a law   2. the law or laws made

33. **leg·is·la·tor**   *n.* one who legislates

34. **ma·ni·pu·late**   *v.* **–la·ted, –la·ting** 1. influence or control cleverly, shrewdly, or deviously 2. hold something in one's hands and move it

35. **ma·ni·pu·la·tion**   *n.* skillful handling or operation, clever or dishones management or control

36. **nav·i·gate**   *v.* **–ga·ted, –ga·ting** 1. travel on water   2. direct carefully and safely

37. **nav·i·ga·tion**   *n. 1.* the science of locating the position and plotting the course of ships   2. the guidance of a ship or airplane

38. **nav·i·ga·tor**   *n.* one who navigates

39. **nar·rate**   *v.* **–ra·ted, –ra·ting** 1. to recite or give a detailed account of   2. provide commentary (for a film or play)

40. **nar·ra·tion**   *n.* telling of a story or of happenings

41. **nar·ra·tor**   *n.* one who narrates

42. **ob·li·gate**   *v.* **–ga·ted, –ga·ting** 1. force somebody to do something   2. cause to be indebted

43. **ob·li·ga·tion**   *n.* a legal or moral responsibility

44. **par·ti·ci·pate**   *v.* **–pa·ted, –pa·ting** to have or take a share with others (in an activity, etc.)

45. **par·ti·ci·pa·tion**   *n.* the act of sharing in the activities of a group; involvement

46. **sep·a·rate**   *v.* **–ra·ted, –ra·ting** 1. act as a barrier   2. to force or pull apart   3. to divide

47. **sep·a·ra·tion**   *n. 1.* a dividing or coming apart   2. an arrangement by which a husband and wife live apart by agreement or court decree

Practicing the words
A. Complete each pair of sentences with a noun form (**ion**) and a verb form (**ate**) of the same word.
Also write the abbreviation of which part of speech it is after writing the sentence.

1. Judges filled out _____ forms on each contestant. _____

   The teacher will _____ the results of the tests. _____

2. The soldier was awarded a _____ for bravery. _____

   Who will volunteer to _____ the gym for the party? _____

3. The lonely forest gave the campers a feeling of _____. _____

   One avalanche can _____ that mountain village for months. _____

4. The magician baffled us with the clever _____ of his props. _____

   The machine operator must _____ those levers in a certain order. _____

5. Can you _____ the boat between those rocks? _____

   The co-pilot took over the _____ of the airplane. _____

6. Does the furnace _____ generate enough heat? _____

   What music did people in our grandparents' _____ listen to? _____

7. The math teacher wrote the _____ on the whiteboard. _____

   Would you _____ being happy with being successful? _____

8. All students are expected to _____ in the class project. _____

   _____ in the sports program is voluntary. _____

9. How does one _____ the egg white from the yolk? _____

   They hung the curtain to make a _____ between men and women. _____

10. Sometimes people _____ after eating cholent on Shabbos afternoon. _____

    Bears usually find a cave for their winter _____. _____

11. Jews commemorate the 6 days of _____ by keeping Shabbos. _____

    Shimshy and Boruch will _____ a new shlok for Sukkos this year. _____

12. New _____ about how to vote is a topic full of contention. _____

    Congress will _____ a new law prohibiting vaping in public. _____

29

13. The First Ammendment protects Americans' right to _____. _____

    The _____ responds to the chazzan when he recites kaddish. _____

14. The pilot needed assistance of his instruments for _____ of the flight. _____

    A kosher Waze device can help you _____ your way back home. _____

15. Shmerel's mother can help you _____ your next event. _____

    With everyone's _____, the sukkah was erected in no time. _____

16. The play director hired a professional for the _____. _____

    Your essay should _____ the family trip during summer vacation. _____

17. Sometimes the Ballooner Rebbe needs a pump to _____ balloons. _____

    Since Corona, there is _____, which signifies that Moshiach near. _____

18. When faced with _____, remember that Hashem controls everything. _____

    My mother told me not to _____ my younger sister. _____

19. The tower's shakiness spurred an _____ order by the fire department. _____

    When a hurricane nears, officials _____ tourists from the beaches. _____

20. Four nations seem to contend for _____ over the world. _____

    In the future, Hashem's Kingdom will _____ the entire world. _____

B. Unscramble the nouns in the first column. First find and circle the **ion** ending. It is not scrambled. Then unscramble the verbs in the second column. Begin by circling the **ate** ending.

1. ticapionartpi _____   1. atetrir _____

2. gotbionail _____   2. sliateo _____

3. etihbnriona _____   3. rodcoatein _____

4. nimdionoat _____   4. gatergeocn _____

5. artegenion _____   5. sigateell _____

6. utqionea _____   6. atelogbi _____

7. vucionatea _____   7. modinate _____

8. tionrapase _____   8. aterec _____

9. vanigionat _____   9. panimateul _____

10. veautliona _____   10. breatehin _____

11. rarionata _____   11. uateqe _____

12. attionirri _____   12. ateatipcipr _____

13. asionloti _____   13. ecateord _____

14. taionocridon _____   14. eregaten _____

15. iongoegncrtar _____   15. auveatec _____

16. elialiongst _____   16. prateeas _____

17. aretionc _____   17. iatevagn _____

18. nplaionatimu _____   18. liatenf _____

19. crdionaeot _____   19. ulateeav _____

20. liafiont _____   20. anaterr _____

31

C.
Many words that end with **ate** have a noun form that ends with **or**: narrate – narrator. Add **or** to some of the **ate** verbs from your spelling list to make nouns that match the definitions below. Then add **'s** to each noun to make a possessive form that completes each phrase. The possessive form of a noun shows that something belongs to it.

1. makes laws   _____ a _____ vote

2. tells a story   _____ the _____ voice

3. finds the way   _____ a _____ map

4. produces energy   _____ the _____ power

5. brings into being   _____ the _____ masterpiece

6. brings order   _____ the _____ plan

7. makes attractive   _____ the _____ fabrics

Now expand five of the phrases into complete sentences.

_____

_____

_____

_____

_____

_____

_____

_____

D. Complete each sentence with a spelling word.

1. Both sides of an __ __ __ __ __ __ __ __ must be equal.

2. To ensure __ __ __ __ __ __ __ __ __ __ of men and women, a mechitzah is placed.

3. His essay was a __ __ __ __ __ __ __ __ __ of the entire trip.

4. If you enhance the __ __ __ __ __ __ __ __ __ __ of your Sukkah, you are performing hiddur mitzvah.

5. When animals go into winter __ __ __ __ __ __ __ __ __ __ __, their body rests in an inactive state.

6. With new __ __ __ __ __ __ __ __ __ __ against vaping about to take effect, I know someone who is going out of business.

7. In the times of chevlei Moshiach we can expect __ __ __ __ __ __ __ __ __, as the Mishnah says that יוקר יאמיר – prices will significantly increase.

8. When faced with __ __ __ __ __ __ __ __ __ __, I remind myself that כעס is a terrible עבירה.

9. It is a positive __ __ __ __ __ __ __ __ __ __ to hear the shofar blown on Rosh Hashanah.

10. The ג"י מידות may only be said with a __ __ __ __ __ __ __ __ __ __ __ __ __ – when a complete minyan is present.

11. As the Yomim Norayim approach, __ __ __ __ __ __ __ __ __ __ of our conduct throughout the year is expected.

12. On Rosh Hashanah we celebrate the __ __ __ __ __ __ __ __ of man, when Hashem's Kingship began.

13. A map used to be essential for __ __ __ __ __ __ __ __ __ __, before the GPS became so widespread.

14. With the entire family's __ __ __ __ __ __ __ __ __ __ __ __, we erected our sukkah in no time at all.

15. As the hurricane approached, mandatory __ __ __ __ __ __ __ __ __ forced the vacationers

away from the shore.

16. My grandparents were from a different __ __ __ __ __ __ __ __ __ __, they never owned a

computer, let alone used a cell phone.

17. Students use all sorts of __ __ __ __ __ __ __ __ __ __ __ to avoid being responsible for

their behavior.

18. America, China, Russia, and Iran seem to contend for __ __ __ __ __ __ __ __ __ __ over the

world.

19. Everyone's __ __ __ __ __ __ __ __ __ __ __ __ is necessary to get the work done properly.

20. Unvaccinated people are sometimes kept in __ __ __ __ __ __ __ __ __ after having been

exposed to contagious diseases like measles.

Spelling Lesson 4

Key Concepts
- base word
- prefix

A **base word** is a word before any changes have been made.

A prefix is a group of letters added to the beginning of a word to change its meaning. This might alter the pronunciation of the word, but its spelling should not change.

Understanding the meaning of basic prefixes will help you understand the meaning of many new words. In addition, recognizing the prefix can help you remember how to spell the word.

Lesson Spelling Rule: A prefix can be added directly to a base word to form a new word with a different meaning. The spelling of the base word does not change when a prefix is added.

Prefixes used in this lesson, together with their meanings:
- re- means back, again, anew
- ex- means beyond, out of, thoroughly, former, previous
- in- means in, into, within, on, toward; no, not, without
- de- means away from; reverse the action of
- pro- means before in place or time; forward or ahead; supporting, favoring
- dis- means away, apart; not; opposite of
- sub- means under, beneath; lower in position; to a lesser degree; by division into smaller parts
- pre- means before in time, place or rank
- con- means with, together, or all together; very or very much
- per- means throughout; thoroughly

1. RE + STRAIN	=	RESTRAIN
2. RE + QUEST	=	REQUEST
3. EX + PLAIN	=	EXPLAIN
4. EX + CHANGE	=	EXCHANGE
5. IN + JUSTICE	=	INJUSTICE
6. IN + CORPORATE	=	INCORPORATE
7. DE + NOTATION	=	DENOTATION
8. DE + MERIT	=	DEMERIT
9. PRO + CLAIM	=	PROCLAIM
10. PRO + PORTION	=	PROPORTION
11. DIS + SATISFIED	=	DISSATISFIED
12. DIS + CHARGE	=	DISCHARGE
13. SUB + STANDARD	=	SUBSTANDARD
14. SUB + COMMITTEE	=	SUBCOMMITTEE
15. PRE + HISTORIC	=	PREHISTORIC
16. PRE + JUDGE	=	PREJUDGE
17. CON + TRIBUTE	=	CONTRIBUTE
18. CON + GENIAL	=	CONGENIAL
19. PER + FUME	=	PERFUME
20. PER + MISSION	=	PERMISSION

Pay attention to the spelling words.

1. What ten prefixes have been added to form spelling words? _____ _____ _____

_____ _____ _____ _____ _____ _____ _____

2. Were the prefixes added to complete words? _____

3. Does the spelling of the prefix or the base word change when the two are joined? _____

4. Does the meaning of the word change when the prefix is added? _____

> A prefix can be added directly to a base word to form a new word with a different meaning. The spelling of the base word does not change when a prefix is added.

Spelling Dictionary

1. **change**   *n.* a difference   *–v.* **changed, chan·ging** to make different
2. **charge**   *n.* the quantity that an apparatus is fitted to hold
    –v. **charged, char·ging** to completely fill
3. **claim**   *n.* a request; a demand; something claimed   *–v.* **claimed, claim·ing** demand, to ask for
4. **com·mit·tee**   *n.* a group of persons appointed to perform some service or function
5. **con·gen·ial**   *adj.* similar, compatible; suited to one's needs, mood, or nature; agreeable
6. **con·tri·bute**   *v.* **–bu·ted, –bu·ting** to give to a common fund, as for charity, education, etc.
7. **cor·por·ate**   *adj.* 1. forming, of, or belonging to a corporation   2. united or combined into one
8. **de·mer·it**   *n.* a fault; mark recorded against someone for poor conduct or work
9. **de·no·ta·tion**   *n.* the basic literal meaning of a word
10. **dis·charge**   *v.* **–charged, –char·ging** to relieve of a burden; to release or remove; to let out
11. **dis·sat·is·fied**   *adj.* displeased
12. **ex·change**   *v.* **–changed, –chan·ging** to give or receive another thing for
    –n. a giving or taking of one thing for another
13. **ex·plain**   *v.* **–plained, –plain·ing** to make plain or understandable
14. **fume**   *n.* smokelike or vaporous exhalation
15. **gen·ial**   *adj.* sympathetically cheerful
16. **his·tor·ic**   *adj.* well-known in history
17. **in·cor·po·rate**   *v.* **–ra·ted, –ra·ting** 1. to bring together into a whole, merge   2. to form into a corporation
18. **in·jus·tice**   *n.* an unjust act, injury
19. **judge**   *n.* a person qualified to decide; to pass judgment
    –v. **judged, jud·ging** 1. to determine the result   2. to form a critical opinion of
20. **jus·tice**   *n.* lawfulness
21. **mer·it**   *n.* claim to excellence   *–v.* to deserve, be worthy of
22. **miss·ion**   *n.* 1. a group acting on behalf of government   2. a specific task that person(s) was sent to perform
23. **no·ta·te**   *v.* **–ta·ted, –ta·ting** the act of making notes in writing
24. **no·ta·tion**   *n.* written note
25. **per·miss·ion**   *n.* formal consent
26. **per·fume**   *n.* fragrance; a substance producing a pleasing odor
27. **plain**   *adj.* clear, without extras
28. **por·tion**   *n.* part of a whole   *–v.* to divide
29. **pre·his·tor·ic**   *adj.* of the period before recorded history
30. **pre·judge**   *v.* **–judged, –jud·ging** to judge beforehand, or before one knows enough to judge
31. **pro·claim**   *v.* **–claimed, –claim·ing** to announce to the public officially

32. **pro·por·tion**   *n.* comparative relation of one thing to another; pleasing arrangement; balance of parts

33. **quest**   *v.* **ques·ted, ques·ting** to search

34. **re·quest**   *v.* **–ques·ted, –ques·ting** to ask for (esp. in a polite way) —*n.* an asking for something, something asked for

35. **re·strain**   *v.* to hold back from action, to curb, to limit, restrict

36. **sa·tis·fied**   *adj.* content

37. **stan·dard**   *n.* 1. basis of comparison   2. ethics established by authority or custom *adj.* conforming to custom

38. **strain**   *v.* **strained, strain·ing** to exert, use to the utmost; injure or hurt

39. **sub·stan·dard**   *adj.* below some standard set by law or custom

40. **sub·com·mit·tee**   *n.* any of the small committees with special duties into which a main committee may be divided

41. **tri·bute**   *n.* gift; forced payment; tax

Practicing the words
A. Write the spelling word that contains each smaller word. Do not repeat a word.

1. mitt

    _____

2. just

    _____

3. aim

    _____

4. miss

    _____

5. sat

    _____

6. rate

    _____

7. but

    _____

8. on

    _____

9. it

    _____

10. his

    _____

11. port

    _____

12. rain

    _____

13. stand

    _____

14. not

    _____

15. char

    _____

16. lain

    _____

B. Crossword

Complete the crossword puzzle below

Across
6. Merge; combine with something else
8. To give
9. Exact meaning of a word
11. Ask for

Down
1. Trade
2. Consent
3. To form an opinion before having facts
4. A mark put against someone
5. Not content
7. Agreeable
10. Pleasing fragrance

C. Working with prefixes

Write at least one meaning for each of the following prefixes. Then write the spelling words that match the definitions below. To make it easier for you, the underlined word(s) correspond to the prefix.

per _____   re _____

ex _____   pre _____

pro _____   dis _____

in _____   sub _____

con _____   de _____

1. the opposite of satisfied   _____

2. hold back   _____

3. before recorded history   _____

4. combine into one   _____

5. below a measure of quality   _____

6. announce before the public   _____

7. an act that is not just   _____

8. to clear out confusion   _____

D. Fill in the following sentences with the appropriate spelling words.

1. The flowers' __ __ __ __ __ __ __ scented the night air.

2. How would you __ __ __ __ __ __ __ this Tosafos?

3. The prosecutors demanded a sentence that was beyond __ __ __ __ __ __ __ __ __ __ __.

4. The lawmakers need to address this __ __ __ __ __ __ __ __ __.

5. He was going to __ __ __ __ __ __ __ __ __ __ __ my shtickel in his new sefer.

6. The __ __ __ __ __ __ __ __ __ __ __ __ reported to the entire group.

7. A bad middah is a type of __ __ __ __ __ __ __ .

8. As you grow up, you must learn to __ __ __ __ __ __ __ __ your anger.

9. In olden days a town crier used to __ __ __ __ __ __ __ __ the news.

10. Let's __ __ __ __ __ __ __ __ telephone numbers.

11. The teacher is __ __ __ __ __ __ __ __ __ __ __ __ with lousy excuses.

12. The exact meaning is a word's __ __ __ __ __ __ __ __ __ __.

13. Those chimneys __ __ __ __ __ __ __ __ thick smoke.

14. We __ __ __ __ __ __ __ your presence at our simchah.

15. In a dollar store, you often find __ __ __ __ __ __ __ __ __ __ __ goods sold for discount.

16. Parental __ __ __ __ __ __ __ __ __ __ is required for the field trip.

17. We have very little reliable information about __ __ __ __ __ __ __ __ __ __ __ times.

18. It is unfair to __ __ __ __ __ __ __ __ another's actions.

19. Feel free to __ __ __ __ __ __ __ __ __ __ your ideas for consideration.

20. We are lucky to have such __ __ __ __ __ __ __ __ __ neighbors.

E. Build a word pyramid by following the code. Using your knowledge of prefixes, find the four pyramid words that match the definitions.

The word **claim** means "to call for or demand."

1. to "call out" in public

_____

2. to demand the return of something

_____

3. to "call out" as not being one's own

_____

4. shouted out loud

_____

5. unwanted

_____

			C	L	A	I	M			
	8	3	C	L	A	I	M			
7	8	6	C	L	A	I	M	3	2	
	3	12	C	L	A	I	M	3	2	
	11	5	C	L	A	I	M			
2	4	9	C	L	A	I	M			
			C	L	A	I	M	1	5	10

A	D	E	I	N	O	P	R	S	T	U	X
1	2	3	4	5	6	7	8	9	10	11	12

F. Build another word pyramid by following the code. See if you can find the four pyramid words that match the definitions.

The word **tribute** means "something given or assigned."

1. can be "assigned" to a particular person or place

_____

2. to give money to

_____

3. punishment given for a wrong

_____

4. a characteristic "assigned to" a person

_____

		T	R	I	B	U	T	E			
	1	12	T	R	I	B	U	T	E		
3	9	8	T	R	I	B	U	T	E		
4	6	11	T	R	I	B	U	T	E		
		T	R	I	B	U	T	1	10	13	
	10	5	T	R	I	B	U	T	6	9	8
	1	12| T	R	I	B	U	T	1	2	7	5

A	B	C	D	E	I	L	N	O	R	S	T	Y
1	2	3	4	5	6	7	8	9	10	11	12	13

G. Prefixes

You can discover or make up your own new words by combining prefixes with base words. Using your understanding of the prefixes and the base words, pick at least one word from each of the following lists and write a definition for it. If you picked a word to which you do not know the definition, get creative and manufacture your own!

- exSTRAIN   inSTRAIN   deSTRAIN   proSTRAIN   disSTRAIN
  subSTRAIN   preSTRAIN   conSTRAIN   erSTRAIN

- exQUEST   inQUEST   deQUEST   proQUEST   disQUEST
  subQUEST   preQUEST   conQUEST   rQUEST

- rePLAIN   inPLAIN   dePLAIN   proPLAIN   disPLAIN
  subPLAIN   prePLAIN   conPLAIN   rPLAIN

- reCHANGE   inCHANGE   deCHANGE   proCHANGE   disCHANGE
  subCHANGE   preCHANGE   conCHANGE   rCHANGE

- reJUSTICE   exJUSTICE   deJUSTICE   proJUSTICE   disJUSTICE
  subJUSTICE   preJUSTICE   conJUSTICE   perJUSTICE

- reCORPORATE   exCORPORATE   deCORPORATE   proCORPORATE
  disCORPORATE   subCORPORATE   preCORPORATE   conCORPORATE
  perCORPORATE

- reNOTATION   exNOTATION   inNOTATION   proNOTATION
  disNOTATION   subNOTATION   preNOTATION   conNOTATION
  perNOTATION

- reMERIT   exMERIT   inMERIT   proMERIT   disMERIT
  subMERIT   preMERIT   conMERIT   perMERIT

- reCLAIM   exCLAIM   inCLAIM   deCLAIM   disCLAIM
  subCLAIM   preCLAIM   conCLAIM   perCLAIM

- rePORTION   exPORTION   inPORTION   dePORTION   disPORTION
  subPORTION   prePORTION   conPORTION   perPORTION

- reSATISFIED   exSATISFIED   inSATISFIED   deSATISFIED   proSATISFIED
  subSATISFIED   preSATISFIED   conSATISFIED   perSATISFIED

- reCHARGE   exCHARGE   inCHARGE   deCHARGE   proCHARGE
  subCHARGE   preCHARGE   conCHARGE   perCHARGE

- reSTANDARD   exSTANDARD   inSTANDARD   deSTANDARD
  proSTANDARD   disSTANDARD   preSTANDARD   conSTANDARD
  perTANDARD

- reCOMMITTEE   exCOMMITTEE   inCOMMITTEE   deCOMMITTEE
  proCOMMITTEE   disCOMMITTEE   preCOMMITTEE   conCOMMITTEE
  perCOMMITTEE

- reHISTORIC   exHISTORIC   inHISTORIC   deHISTORIC   proHISTORIC
  disHISTORIC   subHISTORIC   conHISTORIC   perHISTORIC

- reJUDGE   exJUDGE   inJUDGE   deJUDGE   proJUDGE
  disJUDGE   subJUDGE   conJUDGE   perJUDGE

- reTRIBUTE   exTRIBUTE   inTRIBUTE   deTRIBUTE   proTRIBUTE
  disTRIBUTE   subTRIBUTE   preTRIBUTE   perTRIBUTE

- reGENIAL   exGENIAL   inGENIAL   deGENIAL   proGENIAL
  disGENIAL   subGENIAL   preGENIAL   perGENIAL

- reFUME   exFUME   inFUME   deFUME   proFUME
  disFUME   subFUME   conFUME   preFUME

- reMISSION   exMISSION   inMISSION   deMISSION   proMISSION
  disMISSION   subMISSION   conMISSION   preMISSION

Key Concepts
- root
- prefix
- suffix

A **root** is a word part that cannot stand alone. It must be joined to other parts to form a word, either a prefix or a suffix. Sometimes, it will be joined with both a prefix and suffix to form a word. The final meaning of the word will usually be a combination of the meaning of the prefix, suffix, and root. When the same root is joined to different prefixes, their meaning is different enough from each other that they are not related words even though they may still have a similar meaning.

A **prefix** is a group of letters added to the beginning of a word to change its meaning. This might alter the pronunciation of the word, but its spelling should not change. A prefix can also be joined before a root to form a word.

A **suffix** is a word ending that changes the use of a word or its function. It can also be joined after a root to form a word.

When you understand the meanings of common prefixes, suffixes, and roots you can easily decipher the meanings of new words you encounter.

Prefix	+	Root	+	Suffix		Complete Word
re		flect		ion	=	reflection

Lesson Spelling Rule: A root can be joined with many different prefixes. Changing the prefix forms a word with a different meaning.

Roots used in this lesson, together with their meanings:
- CESS means to yield, or to move – related words have to do with moving or giving up
- STITUTE means to stand – related words have to do with conceptual STANDING in the sense of right to exist, rather than the act of staying straight up
- FLECT means to bend
- SPIRE means breath[10] – related words have to do with air or ideas
- HIBIT means to hold – refers to physical holding, as well as to supporting, showing, or maintaining
- JECT means to throw
- SUADE means to urge
- SUME means to take up, or to add – refers to physically adding, as in sums of addition; as well as to taking on ideas.

The root ject means "to throw."
> deject = to throw down, depress
> reject = to throw back
> project = to throw forth or forward

---

10 Not to be confused with the word **spire**, which means a tall narrow part of a building. **SPIRIT** comes from this root, and it often has a metaphorical aspect in addition to the physical act of breathing.

1.	RE + CESS + ION	=	RECESSION
2.	PRO + CESS + ION	=	PROCESSION
3.	CON + CESS + ION	=	CONCESSION
4.	CON + STITUTE + ION	=	CONSTITUTION
5.	SUB + STITUTE + ION	=	SUBSTITUTION
6.	IN + STITUTE + ION	=	INSTITUTION
7.	RE + FLECT + ION	=	REFLECTION
8.	IN + FLECT + ION	=	INFLECTION
9.	PER + SPIRE	=	PERSPIRE
10.	IN + SPIRE	=	INSPIRE
11.	EX + HIBIT	=	EXHIBIT
12.	IN + HIBIT	=	INHIBIT
13.	PRO + HIBIT	=	PROHIBIT
14.	DE + JECT + ION	=	DEJECTION
15.	RE + JECT + ION	=	REJECTION
16.	PRO + JECT + ION	=	PROJECTION
17.	PER + SUADE	=	PERSUADE
18.	DIS + SUADE	=	DISSUADE
19.	PRE + SUME	=	PRESUME
20.	CON + SUME	=	CONSUME

Pay attention to the spelling words.

1. Before the prefixes and suffixes are added, are the letter group complete words? _____

2. A word part that must be joined to other word parts to for a complete word is called a _____.

3. How many different roots are used in the word list? _____

4. How many words are formed from these roots? _____

5. Do **reject**, **deject**, and **project** have the same root? _____

6. Do they have the same meaning? _____

> A root can be joined with many different prefixes. Changing the prefix forms a word with a different meaning.

Spelling Dictionary

1. **con·cede**   *v.* **–ce·ded, –ce·ding** to give up
2. **con·ces·sion**   *n.* 1. a conceding, or giving in   2. the right to sell food, parking space ect. on the landlord's premises
3. **con·sti·tute**   *v.* **–tu·ted, –tu·ting** to form or compose
4. **con·sti·tu·tion** *n.* 1. the act of forming or establishing something   2. the way that something is formed   3. law determining the fundamental principles of a government
5. **con·sume**   *v.* **–sumed, –sum·ing** 1. to use up; spend or waste (time, energy, money, etc.)   2. to eat or drink up; devour
6. **de·ject**   *v.* **–jec·ted, –jec·ting** lower someone's spirits; make downhearted
7. **de·jec·tion**   *n.* a being dejected or sad; depression
8. **dis·suade**   *v.* **–sua·ded, –sua·ding** to turn (a person) aside (*from* a course of action, etc.) by persuasion or advice
9. **ex·hi·bit**   *v.* **–bi·ted, –bi·ting** to show; display   *–n.* a show; display
10. **in·flect**   *v.* **–flec·ted, –flec·ting** to change the tone of one's voice
11. **in·flec·tion**   *n.* a change in tone or pitch of the voice
12. **in·hi·bit**   *v.* **–bi·ted, –bi·ting** to hold back or keep from some action, feeling, etc. [a person *inhibited* by fear]
13. **in·spire**   *v.* **–spired, –spi·ring** to influence, stimulate, or urge, as to some creative or effective effort
14. **in·sti·tute**   *v.* **–tu·ted, –tu·ting** to establish, or to set up
15. **in·sti·tu·tion** *n.* 1. an establishes law, custom, practice, etc.   2. an organization having a social, educational, or religious purpose, as a school, reformatory, etc.   3. the act of establishing   4. [Colloq.[11]] a person or thing long established
16. **per·spire**   *v.* **–spired, –spi·ring** to give forth {a characteristic salty moisture) through the pores of the skin; sweat
17. **per·suade**   *v.* **–sua·ded, –sua·ding** to cause to do or believe something, esp. by reasoning, urging, etc.
18. **pre·sume**   *v.* **–sumed, –sum·ing** 1. to take upon oneself without permission; venture [I wouldn't *presume* to tell you what to do]   2. to take for granted; suppose [I *presume* you know the risk you are taking]
19. **pro·cess**   *n.* 1. a particular course of action intended to achieve a result   2. a natural outgrowth from an organism   *–v.* **-cessed, -cess·ing** 1. deal with in a routine way   2. march in a procession
20. **pro·ces·sion**   *n.* a number of persons or things moving forward as in a parade, in an orderly way
21. **pro·ject**   *v.* **–jec·ted, –jec·ting** 1. extend out or protrude in space   2. put out or send forth   3. project onto a screen   *–n.* an undertaking

---

11 Colloq. stands for colloquialism. It is means informal speech.

22. **pro·jec·tion** *n.* 1. something that projects or juts out 2. a prediction based on known facts, data, etc.

23. **pro·hi·bit** *v.* **–bi·ted, –bi·ting** 1. to refuse to permit; forbid by law or by an order [smoking is *prohibited* in the building] 2. to prevent; hinder

24. **re·cess** *n.* 1. a hidden or inner place 2. a temporary halting of work, study, etc. *v.* **-cessed, -cess·ing** to move back or to leave

25. **re·ces·sion** *n.* 1. a going backward; withdrawal 2. a departing procession 3. a falling off of business activity

26. **re·flect** *v.* **–flec·ted, –flec·ting** 1. to throw or bend back 2. show an image of

27. **re·flec·tion** *n.* 1. anything reflected or given back, such as an image 2. the act of bending back 3. serious thought; contemplation

28. **re·ject** *v.* **–jec·ted, –jec·ting** 1. to refuse to take, agree to, use, believe, etc. 2. to discard as worthless or below standard

29. **re·jec·tion** *n.* 1. the act of rejecting something 2. the state of being rejected

30. **sub·sti·tute** *v.* **–tu·ted, –tu·ting** to put in place of another, switch *—n.* a person or thing that takes the place of another

31. **sub·sti·tu·tion** *n.* the substituting of one person or thing for another

So how do the word parts add up to the definitions? If you consider the meanings of the prefixes together with the roots, it isn't too difficult to decipher them.

RECESS The root CESS means to yield, or to move, so it has to do with moving or giving up. The prefix RE means back, or again, so to RECESS is to move back or leave. A RECESSION is the act or period of moving back.

PROCESS The root CESS means to yield, or to move, so it has to do with moving or giving up. The prefix PRO means forward, earlier, or in support of, so to PROCESS is to move forward. A PROCESSION is the act of moving forward.

CONCESSION The root CESS means to yield, or to move, so it has to do with moving or giving up. The prefix CON means with, all together, or very, so to CONCEDE is to give up. A CONCESSION is the act of giving up.

CONSTITUTE The root STITUTE means to stand, so it has to do with staying or existing. The prefix CON means with, all together, or very, so to CONSTITUTE is to make all together. CONSTITUTION is what forms something. One's constitution is what he is verily made up of. A nation's constitution is the set of principles of which it is made.

SUBSTITUTE The root STITUTE means to stand, so it has to do with staying or existing. The prefix SUB means under, lesser than, or smaller, so to SUBSTITUTE is to set something else up instead of, or under, the original. SUBSTITUTION is the act of, or the substance which is, substituting.

INSTITUTE The root STITUTE means to stand, so it has to do with staying or existing. The prefix IN means in, or not, so to INSTITUTE is to establish, or to set up. An INSTITUTION is the act of establishing or the establishment.

REFLECT The root FLECT means to bend. The prefix RE means back, or again, so to REFLECT is to bend back. A REFLECTION is the act of bending back, or the thing which is bent back.

INFLECT The root FLECT means to bend. The prefix IN means in, or not, so to INFLECT is to change the tone of one's voice and an INFLECTION is the tone of one's voice.

PERSPIRE The root SPIRE means breath. The prefix PER means throughout or thoroughly. To PERSPIRE is to sweat – because usually one is breathing heavily when they sweat, and it is as though the breathing is permeating their entire body and breathing out. PERSPIRATION is the noun and refers to the act of perspiring or the sweat itself.

INSPIRE The root SPIRE means breath. The prefix IN means in, or not. To infuse with spirit is to INSPIRE; also to move someone to action. The noun is INSPIRATION.

EXHIBIT The root HIBIT means to hold. The prefix EX means out, beyond, or former. To EXHIBIT is to hold out, to display. The noun is EXHIBITION, and refers to the act of displaying or the display itself.

INHIBIT The root HIBIT means to hold. The prefix IN means in, or not, so to INHIBIT is to hold in, to restrain. INHIBITION is the noun which refers to the act of restraining oneself, or to one's hesitations.

PROHIBIT The root HIBIT means to hold. The prefix PRO means forward, earlier, or in support of. To PROHIBIT is to give instructions earlier that hold people back from doing what is forbidden. The noun is PROHIBITION.

DEJECTION The root JECT means to throw. The prefix DE means under, away, or to undo, so to DEJECT is to feel thrown down, sad, or depressed. The noun is DEJECTION.

REJECTION The root JECT means to throw. The prefix RE means back, or again, so to REJECT is to throw back, to return, or to throw away and discard. The noun is REJECTION.

PROJECTION The root JECT means to throw. The prefix PRO means forward, earlier, or in support of, so to PROJECT is to throw forward. This can be physically, when throwing something; or conceptually, when putting forth an idea. PROJECTION is the noun for throwing forward. It also refers to something which sticks forth more than what is around it.

PERSUADE The root SUADE means to urge. The prefix PER means throughout or thoroughly, so to PERSUADE is to thoroughly urge and convince someone. The noun is PERSUASION.

DISSUADE The root SUADE means to urge. The root DIS means away, to undo. To DISSUADE is to urge someone away from something. The noun is DISSUASION.

PRESUME The root SUME means to take up, or to add. This refers to physically adding, as in sums of addition; as well as to taking on ideas. The root PRE means earlier, before., so to PRESUME is to take on an idea before you have adequate information that supports or proves it. (It is similar to ASSUME, yet it does not bear the same connotation of unsupported doubt – it reflects the likelihood of being borne out in fact.) The noun is PRESUMPTION[12].

CONSUME The root SUME means to take up, or to add. The prefix CON means with, all together, or very. To CONSUME is to take on within oneself: to eat. By extension, it refers to destruction; because fire destroys what it 'eats'. The noun is CONSUMPTION and also refers to tuberculosis, a disease which was often fatal because it led to the patient wasting away: being destroyed by it.

---

12 Notice the spelling change as the suffix is added. See more examples in Lesson 13

Practicing the words

A. Complete each sentence with two spelling words that have the same root and indicate which part of speech it is by its abbreviation. Some words may be used more than once.

1. The writer had feelings of _____ ____ when she received a

   _____ ____ letter from her publisher.

2. The _____ ____ of graduating students into the auditorium was

   solemn, but the _____ ____ of the same group was noisy and

   cheerful.

3. I _____ ____ you know that you should not

   _____ ____ that entire cake.

4. The actor changed the _____ ____ of his voice so that it was a

   better _____ ____ of his character's mood.

5. If I can't _____ ____ you from trying that skating stunt, can I

   at least _____ ____ you to wear knee pads and a helmet?

6. Seeing those runners _____ ____ does not

   _____ ____ me to take up jogging.

7. Moshe and Yehudis bought popcorn at the _____ ____ stand

   while they watched the _____ ____ of marching bands.

8. Writing a _____ ____ was the first order of business after the

   _____ ____ of the new town council.

9. Travel costs may _____ ____ bringing the

   _____ ____ to other countries.

10. One council member called for the _____ ____ of Plan A after

    reading a _____ ____ of the expected costs.

52

B. Proofreading

Mrs. Mixit indulged again in her habit of mixing the wrong prefix with the right root. Help her say what she really means by changing the prefixes of the nine underlined words and writing the words correctly.

Neighbors, what do you think about the constitution of children delivering candy for Mishloach Manos on Purim? Some people believe that we should end this tradition. They try to persuade young people from joining the concession of bell-ringers. They point out that it may not be healthy to presume large amounts of candy and such treats, and that it takes too much time in traffic to deliver to every child's friend. If that is the case, then perhaps each neighborhood could consider a suitable institution for the practice. Maybe children should only give to people who live on their block? On the other hand, most young people would have a feeling of projection if they could not inhibit their clever costumes on Purim. Maybe a period of inflection would perspire parents to find a way to keep Purim fun for all.

1. _____   4. _____   7. _____

2. _____   5. _____   8. _____

3. _____   6. _____   9. _____

C. Fill in the following sentences with the appropriate spelling words.

1. Some people __ __ __ __ __ __ __ a lot even when it is not hot.

2. The הכנסת ספר תורה began with a gala __ __ __ __ __ __ __ __ __.

3. If he loses the race, I look forward to enjoying his __ __ __ __ __ __ __ __ __ __ speech.

4. The pharmacy made a generic __ __ __ __ __ __ __ __ __ __ __ for the brand name medication.

5. The president keeps trying to convince voters that a __ __ __ __ __ __ __ __ __ can only be prevented by him.

6. You can make a קידוש השם if you __ __ __ __ __ __ __ good behavior.

7. Our school is a private __ __ __ __ __ __ __ __ __ __ and can teach Yidishe השקפות.

8. The moon shows a __ __ __ __ __ __ __ __ __ of the sun's light.

9. Rabbi Akiva Eiger was of delicate __ __ __ __ __ __ __ __ __ __ __ __ __.

10. Reading about the Chazon Ish should __ __ __ __ __ __ __ you to greater התמדה.

11. We may not __ __ __ __ __ __ __ חמץ on פסח.

12. Learning מוסר helps you __ __ __ __ __ __ __ your יצר הרע.

13. חז"ל __ __ __ __ __ __ __ __ moving מוקצה on שב"ק.

14. He tried to __ __ __ __ __ __ __ __ me from trying e-cigs.

15. The students expressed __ __ __ __ __ __ __ __ when they found out about the homework.

16. She was prepared to receive a __ __ __ __ __ __ __ __ __ notice when submitting a

job application.

17. The סוכה needed to be adjusted to fit the __ __ __ __ __ __ __ __ __ __ of the roof.

18. Can I __ __ __ __ __ __ __ __ you to join the nightly שיעור?

19. The __ __ __ __ __ __ __ __ __ __ of you voice needs to be changed to a question.

20. We __ __ __ __ __ __ __ all תלמידים want to achieve יראת שמים.

D. Build a word pyramid by following the code. Using your knowledge of prefixes, find the four pyramid words that match the definitions. (Inter – means in between.)

The root **jec** means "to throw."

1. an object thrown through the air

_____

2. thrown back, discarded

_____

3. thrown in between

_____

4. something thrown or jutting forward

_____

						J	E	C				
				10	3	J	E	C	11	3	2	
				2	3	J	E	C	11	5	8	7
				8	1	J	E	C	11	5	7	4
			9	10	8	J	E	C	11	5	8	7
			9	10	8	J	E	C	11	5	6	3
	5	7	11	3	10	J	E	C	11	3	2	
B	D	E	G	I	L	N	O	P	R	T		
1	2	3	4	5	6	7	8	9	10	11		

E. Build another word pyramid by following the code. Using your knowledge of prefixes, find the four pyramid words that match the definitions.

The root **spir** means "breath."

1. A "breathing together", or secret plotting

_____

2. to "breath" enthusiasm into

_____

3. giving forth, or "breathing" moisture through the skin

_____

4. the act of breathing

_____

				S	P	I	R				
		1		S	P	I	R	4			
	6	7		S	P	I	R	4			
9	4	10		S	P	I	R	6	7	5	
11	10	1	7	S	P	I	R	4	3		
2	8	7		S	P	I	R	1	2	12	
10| 4			S	P	I	R	1	11| 6	8	7

A	C	D	E	G	I	N	O	P	R	T	Y
1	2	3	4	5	6	7	8	9	10	11	12

56

Review:

Roots used in this lesson, together with their meanings:

- CESS means to yield, or to move – related words have to do with moving or giving up
  - additional words with the root **cess**: accession, excess, precess
- STITUTE means to stand – related words have to do with conceptual STANDING in the sense of right to exist, rather than the act of staying straight up
  - additional words with the root **stitute**: restitution, destitute
- FLECT means to bend
  - additional words with the root **flect**: deflection, deflect
- SPIRE means breath – related words have to do with air or ideas
  - Additional words with the root **spire**: expire, expiration, conspire
- HIBIT means to hold – refers to physical holding, as well as to supporting, showing, or maintaining
  - Additional words with the root **hibit**: disinhibit
- JECT means to throw
  - Additional words with the root **ject**: subject, subjection, conject, conjecture
- SUADE means to urge
  - Additional words with the root **suade**: persuasion, suasion, unpersuade
- SUME means to take up, or to add – refers to physically adding, as in sums of addition; as well as to taking on ideas.
  - Additional words with the root **sume**: consumption, subsume, resume, resumption

Key Concepts
- compound word
- changes in language over time
- contraction
- hyphen
- apostrophe

A **compound word** is when two words are connected without any spelling changes to either word. **Compound** means having more than one part. Compound words are sometimes written as a single word, with no space in between them. Other times, they are hyphenated – joined with a hyphen in between them. Language can be really confusing in that way. Not only that, language changes over time and the way words are spelled shifts. How are you supposed to know which words are spelled which way? Generally, when a compound word begins to be used, it needs a hyphen to connect them to prevent confusion because not everyone recognizes the compound word. After a long period of usage, the hyphen begins to be dropped and the compound word is written as a single word. You can consult a dictionary to determine the correct spelling for a compound word. If a good dictionary does not contain an entry for the compound word, you can assume the word is still relatively new and still requires a hyphen.

What is a hyphen, anyway? A **hyphen** is a horizontal line in middle of the height of the line, similar to a dash, but has no space before an after it. It is used the same way you would use a letter in middle of the word – you would not leave an extra space in middle of the word. The difference between a hyphen and a dash is that the dash always has a space both before and after it. The dash is not used as a letter, it is used as a punctuation mark in middle of a sentence. A hyphen is used as a letter – to connect parts of a word to form a single word.

A **contraction** is formed when parts of a word are left out. To contract means to shrink. A longer word can drop some of its letters to form a contraction. Sometimes multiple words drop letters and combine to form a single contraction. But how is the reader to know that you dropped some of the letters? You indicate the missing letters with an apostrophe. Beware a common error – the apostrophe does not necessarily go between the original words, it only goes in place of the missing letters.

An **apostrophe** is a mark that looks like a floating comma. It hovers just above the letters and indicates that some letters were dropped. It also has another function – to indicate possession of a noun.

Lesson Spelling Rule: Complete words can be combined to form other words in several different ways.
When two words are simply connected with no changes in either word, the word formed is called a compound word.
Words joined by a hyphen are another type of compound word.
When an apostrophe is used to show that one or more letters have been omitted the word is called a contraction.

1. BACK + GROUND	=	BACKGROUND
2. NET + WORK	=	NETWORK
3. SCORE + BOARD	=	SCOREBOARD
4. ROOM + MATE	=	ROOMMATE
5. ELSE + WHERE	=	ELSEWHERE
6. OTHER + WISE	=	OTHERWISE
7. WHO + EVER	=	WHOEVER
8. ANY + ONE	=	ANYONE
9. PROOF + READ	=	PROOFREAD
10. FIRE + PROOF	=	FIREPROOF
11. LIFE + TIME	=	LIFETIME
12. MEAN + WHILE	=	MEANWHILE
13. EVERY + WHERE	=	EVERYWHERE
14. WHEN + EVER	=	WHENEVER
15. SELF + ADDRESSED	=	SELF-ADDRESSED
16. BROTHER + IN + LAW	=	BROTHER-IN-LAW
17. GREAT + AUNT	=	GREAT-AUNT
18. WERE + NOT	=	WEREN'T
19. HAVE + NOT	=	HAVEN'T
20. SHOULD + HAVE	=	SHOULD'VE

Pay attention to the spelling words.

1.   In the first thirteen words, are any changes made when the two smaller words are

joined? _____

2.   Why does **roommate** have two **m's**? _____

3.   Why does **background** have a **g**? _____

4.   In words 15-17, what punctuation is added to join the words? _____

5.   Does the spelling of either word change when the words are joined with the

hyphen? _____

6.   In the last three words, what punctuation is added to join the pairs of words?

_____

7.   What does the apostrophe replace in these words? _____

Complete words can be combined to form other words in several different ways.
When two words are simply connected with no changes in either word, the word formed is
called a compound word.   59
Words joined by a hyphen are another type of compound word.
When an apostrophe is used to show that one or more letters have been omitted the word is
called a contraction.

Spelling Dictionary

1. **air·craft** — *n.* any machine designed for flying, whether heavier or lighter than air; airplane, balloon, helicopter, etc.
2. **an·y·one** — *pron*[13]. any person; anybody
3. **back·ache** — *n.* an ache or pain in the back
4. **back·ground** — *n.* 1. the part of a scene or picture toward the back   2. a position that is unimportant or attracts no attention [try to stay in the *background*]
5. **book·keep·er** — *n.* someone who records the transactions of a business
6. **broad·mind·ed** — *adj.* tolerant of other people's opinions and behavior; not bigoted; liberal
7. **broth·er-in-law** — *n., pl.* **broth·ers**[14]**-in-law** 1. the brother of one's husband or wife   2. the husband of one's sister   3. the husband of the sister of one's wife or husband
8. **else·where** — *adv.* in or to some other place; somewhere else
9. **eve·ry·where** — *adv.* in or to every place
10. **fire·proof** — *adj.* that does not burn
11. **great-aunt** — *n.* a sister of any of one's grandparents
12. **have·n't** — have not
13. **life·time** — *n.* the length of time that one lives
14. **make-be·lieve** — *n.* a pretending or imagining, as in play   —*adj.* pretended; imagined [a *make-believe* friend]
15. **mean·while** — *adv.* at the same time
16. **net·work** — *n.* 1. netting; mesh   2. an interconnected system of things or people   3. (broadcasting) a chain of transmitting station operated as a unit   4. (electronics) a system of interconnected electronic components
17. **oth·er·wise** — *adj.* 1. in another manner; differently   2. in other circumstances; often used as a conjunction meaning "or else" [please help me; *otherwise* I'll be late]
18. **proof·read** — *v.* —**read·ing** to read and mark corrections on
19. **room·mate** — *n.* a person with whom one shares a room or rooms
20. **score·board** — *n.* a large board for posting the score and other details of a game, as in a baseball stadium
21. **self-ad·dressed** — *adj.* addressed to oneself [a *self-addressed* envelope]
22. **should·'ve** — should have
23. **south·west** — *n.* the direction halfway between south and west; 45° west of due south   —*adj.* in, of, to, or from the southwest
24. **two-tone** — *adj.* having two colors
25. **up·date** — *n.* 1. information or facts that update   2. the act of updating —*v.* —**dat·ed, —dat·ing** to bring up to date; make agree with the most recent facts, methods, ideas, etc.

---

13 Pron. stands for pronoun. A pronoun is a part of speech and stands in place of a noun.
14 When a noun is made of a hyphenated compound word, the plural is formed by adding **s** to the main noun instead of the end of the compound word.

26. **well-known**   *adj.* widely or generally known; famous
27. **weren't**   were not
28. **when·ev·er**   *adv.* at whatever time
29. **who·ev·er**   *pron.* any person that; whatever person [*whoever* wins gets
    a prize]

Practicing the words

A. Find the two or three words in each sentence that can be combined to form a compound spelling word. Write the word.

1. Where else should we search for the missing boat? _____

2. Have you ever met the cousin who always writes to you? _____

3. The ground in back of the shed needs clearing. _____

4. The coach wrote the score on the board. _____

5. Is one day this week any more convenient than another? _____

6. My brother hopes to work in a good law office. _____

7. Catching the fish with a net was a lot of work. _____

8. It would be wise to postpone the picnic to some other day. _____

9. The mate to that sock is in the laundry room. _____

10. Meshulam was having the time of his life raking the leaves. _____

11. What proof do you have that fire has more than a single color? _____

12. Sarah's aunt sent her a great box of candy for Chanukah. _____

13. While Yaakov worked very hard, Lavan was very mean by switching his wages.

_____

14. Have you ever wondered when is the ideal time to light Chanukah neiros?

_____

15. I addressed the speech to my very own self. _____

B. Writing

Compose a sentence using each set of spelling words. You may use the words in any order. Write it on the lines after each set.

1. scoreboard, should've, roommate_____

_____

_____

2. anyone, brother-in-law, fireproof_____

_____

_____

3. weren't, proofread, meanwhile_____

_____

_____

4. network, elswhere, whoever_____

_____

_____

5. otherwise, lifetime, great-aunt_____

_____

_____

C. Proofreading

Cross out the misspelled words that appear in Helpful Hymie's newspaper column. Write the words correctly.

Dear Helpful Hymie: My yeshivah roomate is a very risky fellow. He thinks that his tzitzis are fire-proof and likes to dance around and shake them as he burns his fingernails each Friday afternoon. Meenwhile, any-one who watches him is frightened for his safety. We are worried that his tzitzis might catch fire and transfer the flames elsewere. My brother in-law told me that this is pikuach nefesh and I cannot remain silent in the backround doing nothing about it. What do I do?

Cautious and Concerned

Dear C and C: As long as your friend has not yet gotten burned you were'nt too late. I applaud your efforts for public safety. My grate-aunt always used to say that whooever sees danger has to do something about it when-ever they can. You should gather your network of friends and confront the person who is careless with fire. Tell him that there are many opinions that hold it is okay to flush the nails down the toilet. In my entire life-time, I have known only a few people who actually burn theirs. If he still wants to make a fire, he cannot dance around with his strings hanging out. Either he tucks them in or doesn't dance. Otherwize you will have to take matters into your own hands and call the fire department the next time there is danger.

Helpful Hymie

1. _____   5. _____   9. _____

2. _____   6. _____   10. _____

3. _____   7. _____   11. _____

4. _____   8. _____   12. _____

D. Using compound words

The following word parts have been joined the same way to make nonsense words. Using your detective skills, re-match them to make compound or hyphenated compound words. Change only the underlined parts. Cross out each part as you use it. The hyphens are provided for you in the sentences as a hint to help you determine how to combine the words.

1. booktone _____
2. backwest _____
3. broadknown_____
4. airminded _____
5. twodate _____

6. southache _____
7. wellkeeper _____
8. makecraft _____
9. upbelieve _____

Then use each of the new words to complete the following sentences:

1. The tour bus takes visitors to see the homes of _____-_____

   personalities.

2. The _____ found an error in last month's billing.

3. The children were scared, although they knew the story was _____-

   _____.

4. Jeff suffered from a constant _____ after his accident.

5. I couldn't decide between blue or white, so I got _____-_____ shoes.

6. My parents are _____, so I know they will listen to both sides of

   the problem.

7. We got lost by going northeast instead of _____.

8. The _____ seemed sturdy, but Alex was still nervous about flying.

9. Radio stations gave an _____ on the situation every hour.

E. Fill in the blanks with the proper spelling word. A space for a hyphen or an apostrophe has also been marked.

1. You will need to __ __ __ __ __ __ __ __ your essay.

2. The Cheder walls are __ __ __ __ __ __ __ __ __ __.

3. My parents saw many technological changes in their __ __ __ __ __ __ __ __ __.

4. Torah is being learned __ __ __ __ __ __ __ __ __ __ across the globe.

5. My __ __ __ __ __ __ __ __ __ __ passed away about seven years ago.

6. Call me __ __ __ __ __ __ __ __ you are ready.

7. Include a __ __ __ __ __ __ __ __ __ __ __ __ __ __ envelope with your

    application.

8. The __ __ __ __ __ __ __ __ __ __ of the painting was light blue.

9. The Alter of Novardok made a large __ __ __ __ __ __ __ of Yeshivos across

    Russia.

10. The football league has a new electronic __ __ __ __ __ __ __ __ __ __ __.

11. The Rosh Yeshivah was my __ __ __ __ __ __ __ __ __ when we used to be in

    Yeshivah.

12. If the park is full, we will go __ __ __ __ __ __ __ __ __ to play ball.

13. Unless I tell you __ __ __ __ __ __ __ __ __, you should have the work done in

    class.

14. __ __ __ __ __ __ __ needs help should quietly raise their hand.

15. Has __ __ __ __ __ __ completed the essay yet?

16. __ __ __ __ __ __ __ __ __, all we can do is wait for Moshiach.

17. My __ __ __ __ __ __ __ __ __ __ __ __ __ __ __ is a choshuveh Yungerman.

18. I __ __ __ __ __ __ __ yet finished learning Shas.

19. We __ __ __ __ __ __ __ able to join the chaburah.

20. We __ __ __ __ __ __ __ __ __ tried harder to make it on time to seder.

Key Concepts
- compound words
- hyphens
- contractions
- apostrophe
- homonyms
- pronouns
- possessive

A **compound word** is when two words are connected without any spelling changes to either word. **Compound** means having more than one part. Compound words are sometimes written as a single word, with no space in between them. Other times, they are hyphenated – joined with a hyphen between them.

A **hyphen** is a horizontal line in middle of the height of the line, similar to a dash, but has no space before an after it. It is used the same way you would use a letter in middle of the word – you do not leave an extra space in middle of the word.

A **contraction** is formed when parts of a word are left out. To contract means to shrink. A longer word can drop some of its letters to form a contraction. Sometimes multiple words drop letters and combine to form a single contraction. The missing letters are indicated with an apostrophe. Beware a common error – the apostrophe does not necessarily go between the original words, it only goes in place of the missing letters.

An **apostrophe** is a mark that looks like a floating comma. It hovers just above the letters and indicates that some letters were dropped. It also has another function – to indicate possession of a noun.

Homonyms are words that sound alike even though they are not spelled the same way.

A **pronoun** is a word that stands in place of a noun. It is treated by the language nearly identically as a noun (adjectives are used for them) – except for possession, and the same pronoun might be used for different nouns.

Possessive is the form of a noun or pronoun that is used to show ownership – that the noun or pronoun owns something. In this respect there is a difference between nouns and pronouns. Possessive nouns have an apostrophe, pronouns do not.

Lesson Spelling Rule: A hyphen is always used when writing out a fraction or when writing compound numbers from twenty-one to ninety-nine.
Possessive pronouns do not contain an apostrophe.

1. ONE + QUARTER   = ONE-QUARTER
2. TWO + THIRDS   = TWO-THIRDS
3. FOURTEEN
4. NINETY + FOUR   = NINETY-FOUR
5. FORTY + EIGHT   = FORTY-EIGHT
6. THEIR
7. THERE
8. THEY + ARE   = THEY'RE
9. HERE
10. HEAR
11. IT + IS   = IT'S
12. ITS
13. THEIRS
14. THERE + IS or THERE + HAS = THERE'S
15. WHOSE
16. WHO + IS   or WHO + HAS = WHO'S
17. YOU + ARE   = YOU'RE
18. YOUR
19. WEATHER
20. WHETHER

Pay attention to the spelling words.

1. What punctuation mark is used in between the numbers when writing out fractions? _____

2. Is there a space before or after the hyphen? _____

3. What punctuation mark us used to connect the compound numbers?

    _____

4. Is a hyphen used when writing out numbers that are teens?

    _____

5. What change is made in the spelling of the number four when it is multiplied by ten?_____

6. How many sets of similar-sounding words are in this list?

    _____

7. What are sets of similar-sounding words called? _____

> A hyphen is always used when writing out a fraction or when writing compound numbers from twenty-one to ninety-nine. Possessive pronouns do not contain an apostrophe.

69

1. **for·ty-eight**   *n.* the number that is the sum of forty-seven and one –*adj.* being more than orty-seven
2. **four·teen**   *n.* the number that is the sum of thirteen and one –*adj.* being more than thirteen
3. **nine·ty-four**   *n.* the number that is the sum of ninety-three and one –*adj.* being more than ninety-three
4. **hear**   *v.* to perceive or sense (sounds) by the ear
5. **here**   *adv.* at, in, or to this place   –*n.* this place or point
6. **it's**   it is
7. **its**   *pron.* (attributive) belonging to it
8. **one-quar·ter**   *n.* a fourth; one of four equal parts
9. **their**   *adj.* of, belonging to, made by, or done by them [*their* books]
10. **theirs**   *pron.* (attributive) belonging to them
11. **there**   *adv.* at, in, or to that place   –*n.* that place or point [we left *there* at six]
12. **there's**   1. there is   2. there has
13. **they're**   they are
14. **two-thirds**   *n.* two of three equal parts
15. **wea·ther**   *n.* atmospheric conditions comprising of the temperature, wind, sun, clouds, and precipitation   –*v.* face and withstand with courage
16. **whe·ther**   *conj*[15]. used to introduce two or more possibilities
17. **whose**   *pron.* that or those belonging to whom [*whose* is this?] –*adj.* of, belonging to, made by, or done by whom or which [the woman *whose* car was stolen]
18. **who's**   1. who is   2. who has
19. **your**   *pron.* (attributive) belonging to you
20. **you're**   you are

---

15 Conj. stands for conjugation. It is a part of speech that is used to connect or join words or phrases to each other.

Practicing the words
A. Crossword

Complete the crossword puzzle below

Across
3. Listen
4. Belonging to whom
5. Belonging to it
6. Belonging to you
7. Face or withstand with courage
9. This place

Down
1. If
2. 12 plus 2
8. That place

B. Find the two words in each sentence that can be combined to form a compound spelling word. Write the word.

1. Two of the hearty eaters even asked for thirds.

   _____

2. Eight out of forty members were absent from the meeting.

   _____

3. Are you ever going to visit the Kosel Hamaaravi?

   _____

4. Has one got a quarter he can lend me?

   _____

5. Four students scored above ninety on the test.

   _____

6. Is it going to rain today?

   _____

7. Has there been snow this year?

   _____

8. Has someone found out who won the election yet?

   _____

C. Fractions, numbers, and hyphens

The rule for using hyphens when writing out fractions applies only when "translating" the numerical fraction into English words. For example, when writing 2/5 in words, use a hyphen: two-fifths. Even if you are only writing out 1/4, you use a hyphen: one-quarter. However, if you are refering to a single part of a fraction and not writing out the number, then no hyphen is used. For example if you are refering to a half, that is the way it is written – without a hyphen. The same when referring to a quarter, a fifth, or any other such fraction. When you are not writing out the numbers of the fraction, no hyphen is needed.

The rule for compound numbers is that only the numbers from twenty-one to ninety-nine reqire a hyphen (27 = twenty-seven, 53 = fifty-three, etc.).

Ones and teens are written as a single word (1 = one, 2 = two, 6 = six, 11 = eleven, 15 = fifteen, etc.).

When combining hundreds, thousands, or above with ones, teens, or multiples of ten no hyphen is used between them (106 = one hundred six, 4330 = four thousand three hundred thirty, 2,000,006,019 = two billion six thousand nineteen, etc.)

However, the numbers from twenty-one to ninety-nine require a hyphen between them even when combined with higher numbers. (For example: 252 = two hundred fifty-two, s7029 = even thousand twenty-nine, 8,000,044 = eight million forty-four, etc.)

In addition, when compound numbers that require a hyphen are used to count a higher amount they still require a hyphen (3200 = thirty-two hundred, 87,000 = eighty-seven thousand, etc.).

4322 can be written either four thousand three hundred twenty-two
or forty-three hundred twenty-two

Write out the following numbers.
1. 1/8_____

2. 7/13_____

3. 82_____

4. 17_____

5. 212_____

6. 4529_____

_____

7. 2700_____

_____

8. 2/5_____

9. 4/7_____

10. 53,283_____

_____

11. 87,245_____

_____

12. 139,452_____

_____

13. 256,018_____

_____

14. 8/11_____

15. 9/16_____

D. Homonyms

Homonyms are words that sound alike but are spelled differently. Use your understanding of the words to help you complete these sentences with the correct homonyms. It can be very helpful to try and think whether the word is really a contraction of two shorter words. If it is, you can remember to use the apostrophe in place of the missing letters. If it is not a contraction, chances are that there is no need for an apostrophe together with the pronoun.

Complete the following sentences with the correct homonyms:

1. there/they're/their _____ seems no reason _____ happy about

   _____ loss.

2. who's/whose _____ going to the event, and _____ car will he

   use?

3. wear/where _____ in the world can I _____ this silly

   sweater?

4. your/you're _____ cousin is coming to the siyum _____

   making tonight.

5. here/hear If we _____ the shofar from their minyan, it disturbs

   over _____.

6. there/they're/their _____ hats were left _____ in the car with the

   windows open – _____ going to get ruined in the rain.

7. who's/whose _____ going to remove the stinky squash

   _____ smell really disturbs us?

8. wear/where _____ the handsome sweater, and hang up the ugly one

   _____ I told you.

9. your/you're _____ going to be in trouble if you don't put

   _____ clothes away.

10. here/hear   If you _____ the radio over _____, please

     let me know.

11. there/they're/their   _____ looking for _____ car over

     _____.

12. who's/whose   _____ the person _____ portrait is on the

     wall?

13. wear/where   _____ is the shirt I wanted to _____**?**

14. your/you're   _____ ruining _____ new shoes.

15. here/hear   Can you _____ the music over
_____**?**

Associating certain words with one another helps you to remember them. To decide
whether to use **hear** or **here**, for example, associate these words:
     H<u>ear</u> goes with <u>ear</u>.   <u>Here</u> goes with <u>there</u>.
Can you find a way to associate other pairs of homonyms that give you trouble?

E. Fill in the blanks with the appropriate spelling word. The space for a hyphen or an apostrophe has also been marked.

1. If you get __ __ __ __ __ __ __ __ __ __ __ on your test, it isn't too bad.

2. Only __ __ __ __ __ __ __ __ __ __ __ of the class stays for Mishmor.

3. __ __ __ __ __ getting closer to Chanukah.

4. I'm not sure __ __ __ __ __ __ __ there will be mishmor next week.

5. __ __ __ __ __ is a minhag to say selichos on Bahab.

6. Can you __ __ __ __ the chazzan from where you are standing?

7. __ __ __ place is next to the windowsill.

8. The bus popped __ __ __ __ __ ball.

9. __ __ __ __ __ __ going to be a big mesibah.

10. You forgot __ __ __ __ sefer on the bus.

11. __ __ __ __ is the place to light your menorah.

12. Impeaching the president requires a __ __ __ __ __ __ __ __ __ __ majority of the

    Senate to convict.

13. The __ __ __ __ __ __ __ is very comfortable this week.

14. Even in Eretz Yisroel, Rosh Hashanah is __ __ __ __ __ __ __ __ __ __ __ hours.

15. __ __ __ __ __ __ __ nearly always learning Torah.

16. The job of arranging who will lein was __ __ __ __ __.

17. __ __ __ __ __ trying to complete the entire masechta?

18. __ __ __ __ __ ball did I hit out of the yard?

19. A Bar Mitzvah boy is when he enters year __ __ __ __ __ __ __ __.

20. __ __ __ __ __ __ sure to succeed if you daven for siyata dishemaya.

Spelling Lesson 8

Key Concepts
- silent partners
- vowels
- syllables
- mnemonics
- synonyms

Every letter is sometimes silent in the English language. There are a number of letter combinations in which a pair of letters are spelled together but only one of them is pronounced. (Think of the word **combination** – how pronounced is the **b**?) These pairs have a **silent partner** – the letter which is silent.

A vowel is a sound that is made with the throat and mouth opened and can be extended for a while. In other words, a vowel is a נקודה. It functions to help the other sounds of the words come out smoothly and tells you how to pronounce them.

A **syllable** is a word part that has a single vowel sound. It might have a number of vowels (**boat**) or not even a single vowel (dan**g**ling). The key is that it is pronounced as a distinct part of the word separate from the other parts – usually with a separate motion of your mouth. A hint to distinguish the different syllables is to pay attention to your chin as you clearly pronounce the word. Each distinct movement of your chin marks a separate syllable. Sometimes an entire words is a single syllable. This is even true of long words such as **brought**.

Mnemonics is the system of improving memory. A mnemonic device is a memory aid.

A **synonym** is a word that has a similar meaning to another word.

Lesson Spelling Rule: Silent partners are letters which are silent in certain combinations.

1. DESI<u>GN</u>ER
2. ALI<u>GN</u>MENT
3. CAMPAI<u>GN</u>
4. <u>GN</u>AWED
5. INDE<u>BT</u>ED
6. DOU<u>BT</u>FUL
7. <u>PS</u>ALMS
8. <u>PS</u>YCHOLOGY
9. SPA<u>GH</u>ETTI
10. <u>GH</u>ETTO
11. SOLE<u>MN</u>
12. COLU<u>MN</u>
13. CONDE<u>MN</u>
14. AUTU<u>MN</u>
15. QUA<u>LM</u>S
16. CA<u>LM</u>LY
17. PLU<u>MB</u>ING
18. NU<u>MB</u>ED
19. RHYTHMIC
20. RHYMED

Pay attention to the spelling words. Loot at the underlined letters in each word. Only one of the two letters is pronounced. The other letter is a "silent partner." Think about how each word is pronounced.

1. Which letter is silent in each combination? gn _____ bt _____ ps _____

   gh _____ mn _____ lm _____ mb _____ rh _____

2. Write the combinations in which only the **m** is pronounced. _____

   _____ _____

3. Write the letter that is silent in one combination and pronounced in

   another combination. _____

4. Write the letters that are silent in more than one combination. _____

   _____

   | A few consonants are silent in certain combinations. |
   | gn <u>bt</u> ps <u>gh</u> m<u>n</u> <u>l</u>m m<u>b</u> r<u>h</u> |

79

Spelling Dictionary

1. **a·lign·ment**   *n.* arrangement in a straight line
2. **au·tumn**   *n.* season between summer and winter; fall   –
adj. of or like autumn [*autumn* leaves]
3. **be·nign**   *adj.* 1. good-natured [a benign Silent partners (m candidate)rs which are doing little or no harm [a *benign* tumor]   silent in certain combinations.
4. **calm**   *n.* 1. lack of wind or motion; stillness   2. serenity
     –*adj.* 1. still   2. not excited   –**calm·ly**[16] *adv.*
     –**calm·ness** *n.*
SYN[17]. –**calm,** basically applied to the weather, suggests a lack of movement or excitement [a *calm* sea]; **serene** suggests a dignified tranquility, as of a person who is at peace with himself; **peaceful** suggests feedom from disorder or from a show of strong feelings [a *peaceful* gathering]
–**ANT.** –**stormy, agitated**
5. **calm·ly**   *adv.* in a calm manner   –*adj.* 1. still   2. not excited
6. **cam·paign**   *n.* series of organized actions for particular purpose
     –*v.* –**paigned, –paign·ing** to participate in a campaign
7. **col·umn**   *n.* 1. a slender, upright structure; pillar   2. vertical sections of printed matter lying side by side on a page
8. **con·demn**   *v.* –**demned, –demn·ing** 1. to strongly disapprove 2. to convict
9. **con·sign·ment**   *n.* a shipment of goods sent to an agent for sale or safekeeping
10. **de·sign·er**   *n.* person who designs or makes original sketches, patterns, etc.
11. **doubt·ful**   *adj.* 1. not sure   2. questionable
12. **ghet·to**   *n.* any section of a city in which many members of some minority group live, or are forced to live
13. **gnaw**   *v.* **gnawed, gnaw·ing** 1. to bite and wear away bit by bit   2. to torment, as by constant pain, fear, etc.
14. **in·debt·ed**   *adj.* 1. in debt   2. obliged; owing thanks
15. **ma·lign**   *v.* –**ligned, –lign·ing** to say damaging or unfair things about; slander

---

16   The dictionary often lists related words under the entry of the base word. So far, we've only had related words that were also defined. Sometimes the definition is self-understood so long as you know the part of speech. In this case, the dictionary merely states the word in the same font (type of letters) as an entry word and shows which part of speech it is. **Calmly** is an adverb that modifies a verb (it describes the act being done in a calm manner), and **calmness** is a noun – the state of being still.

17   Syn. stands for synonymy, or list of synonyms (words that have similar meanings). See Lesson 11 for more information. Ant. stands for antonyms (the opposite of synonyms).

16. **mort·gage**   *n.* an agreement in which a person borrowing money gives the lender a claim to a certain piece of property as a pledge that the debt will be paid

17. **numb**   *adj.* deprived of the power of feeling or moving; deadened [*numb* with cold]

18. **plumb·ing**   *n.* the pipes and fixtures with which a plumber works

19. **poign·ant**   *adj.* sharply painful to the feelings; drawing forth pity, compassion, etc.

20. **psalms**   *n.* a sacred song or poem

21. **psy·cho·lo·gy**   *n.* the science that studies the mind and the reasons for the ways people think and act

22. **pto·maine**   *n.* any of a class of alkaloid substances, some of which are poisonous, formed in decaying animal or vegetable matter by bacteria

23. **qualms**   *n.* a sudden feeling of uneasiness or doubt

24. **rheu·ma·tism**   *n.* any of various painful conditions in which the joints and muscles become inflamed and stiff

25. **rhyme**   *n.* likeness of sounds at the ends of words or lines of verse   *–v.* **rhymed, rhym·ing** to form a rhyme

26. **rhythm**   *n.* flow or movement having a regularly repeated pattern of accents, beats, etc.

27. **rhythmic**   *adj.* in a manner of rhythm

28. **sold·er**   *n.* a metal alloy used when melted to join or path metal parts or surfaces   *–v.* **–ered, –er·ing** to join or patch (things) with solder

29. **sol·emn**   *adj.* serious; deeply earnest

30. **spa·ghet·ti**   *n.* long, thin strings of pasta

31. **sub·tle**   *adj.* 1. not open or direct; sly; clever [a *subtle* hint] 2. delicate [a *subtle* shade of red]

Practicing the words

A. Syllables

A **syllable** is a word part that has a single vowel sound. It might have a number of vowels (**boat**) or not even a single vowel (dan**g**ling). The key is that it is pronounced as a distinct part of the word separate from the other parts – usually with a separate motion of your mouth. A hint to distinguish the different syllables is to pay attention to your chin as you clearly pronounce the word. Each distinct movement of your chin marks a separate syllable. Sometimes an entire words is a single syllable. This is even true of long words such as **brought**.

1. Write the five one-syllable spelling words.

_____   _____   _____

_____   _____

2. Write the ten two-syllable spelling words. Draw a line between the syllables.

_____   _____   _____

_____   _____   _____

_____   _____

_____   _____

3. Write the four three-syllable words. Draw a line between the syllables.

_____   _____   _____

4. Write the spelling word that remains. _____

   How many syllables does it have? _____

In לשון הקודש a syllable is called either a יתד or a תנועה. In very many of the פיוטים and שירים from the Spanish and African Rishonim, the basis of the verses were written in a format based on these syllables. There is a slight difference between syllables in לשון הקודש and English. In לשון הקודש, the sound of שוא is not a separate syllable, even though it is pronounced with a different movement of the jaw.

A יתד is a syllable that begins with a שוא נא or its assistants (חטף קמץ, חטף פתח, חטף סגול) and continues with the next נקודה. It continues until the following נקודה, which begins the next syllable.

A תנועה is a syllable that begins with a true נקודה on the letter that begins the syllable. It might just be that letter, or up to three letters, all the letters that are pronounced with that נקודה. A שוא cannot begin a תנועה. If it is a שוא נח, it might end the תנועה if the following letter has a new נקודה or a שוא נע; or the תנועה will continue if the following letter is also a שוא נח. [There are two types of שוא נח – one is pronounced and is called נח נראה (visible), the other is not pronounced and is called נח נסתר (hidden). In the word בראשית, the ת is called a נח נראה because its sound is pronounced, but the א and י are נח נסתר because their sounds are not pronounced.]

For example, in the song for Shabbos day, דרור יקרא, the pattern is יתד ושני תנועות. The first stanza of the song is דרור יק·רא לבן עם בת וי·נ·צר·כם כמו ב·בת נעים שמ·כם ולא יש·בת שבו ונו·חו ביום ש·בת. The יתד's have been underlined and bolded. Syllables in a single word have been separated with the dot.

B. Mnemonics

Mnemonics is the system of improving memory. (Cover the first silent letter and say it *nemonics*.)

A mnemonic device is a memory aid.

For example, the word **HOMES** can help you to remember the names of the five Great lakes.

Huron
Ontario
Michigan
Erie
Superior

The word **FACE** tells you the four notes in the spaces of a musical staff.

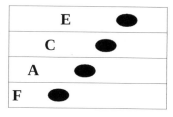

Invent your own mnemonic devices for words that are difficult spelling problems.

Sometimes putting a group of words together in a nonsense sentence or phrase helps you to remember them.

1. Write the four spelling words that have been used in the "silent b" sentence.
Be indebted, doubtful, and numb about plumbing.

_____

2. Make up your own sentence for "silent n" words. solemn, column, condemn,

autumn

_____

_____

3. Make up your own sentence for "silent g" words. designer, campaign, alignment,

gnawed

_____

_____

4. Make up your own sentence for "silent h" words. spaghetti, rhythmic, rhymed

_____

_____

C. Synonyms

Synonyms are words that have a similar meaning to each other. They may have other meanings that are not similar, but the meanings that they share make them synonyms.

The list below contains three spelling words and four of their synonyms. Write a spelling word from the list at the top of each column. Under each spelling word, write its four synonyms.

somber   solemn   uncertain   unsure   serious
skeptical   questionable   serenely   placidly   peacefully
tranquilly   grave   earnest   doubtful   calmly

_____   _____   _____

_____   _____   _____

_____   _____   _____

_____   _____   _____

_____   _____   _____

D. Find nine new silent letter words. Begin with the word sign and find your way out of the maze. Write each word. The beginning of some of the harder words have been provided to help you.

N								
G	E	P	T	O	M	A	I	N
I	G	A	N	T	M	A	L	E
N	A	N	N	S	I	G	I	R
E	G	G	O	S→	I↓	N	G	H
B	T	I	C	N	◄G	M	N	E
R	R	O	P	T	N	E	S	U
E	O	M	E	L	T	B	U	M
D	L	O	S	M	S	I	T	A

sign

1. _____

2. p_____

3. _____

4. s_____

5. _____

6. p_____

7. _____

8. _____

9. _____

Rewrite each sentence, using one of the new words in place of the underlined words. Circle the silent letter.

1. We were moved by the <u>very affecting</u> story.

   _____

2. The stranger gave me a <u>sly, mysterious</u> smile.

   _____

3. Mark is known for his <u>good-natured</u> attitude.

   _____

4. Does the drugstore stock an ointment for <u>stiff muscles</u>?

   _____

5. An electrician should <u>fuse</u> two wires.

   _____

86

6. Which salesperson sold that <u>assigned shipment</u> of food?

   _____

7. The candidate tried to slander his opponent.

   _____

8. Can one contract a case of alkaloid poisoning from mushrooms?

   _____

9. Our neighbors got a second financial agreement on their house.

   _____

E. Fill in the blanks with the appropriate spelling word.

1. His sister is a graphic __ __ __ __ __ __ __ __ and helped him make his business

    card.

2. The lined margin assists the __ __ __ __ __ __ __ __ __ of your words when

    writing a list.

3. The tzedakah __ __ __ __ __ __ __ __ brought in a lot of revenue.

4. Reuvein __ __ __ __ __ __ a spoon when he was lost in thought.

5. I am __ __ __ __ __ __ __ __ __ to the Rov for helping me out.

6. I am __ __ __ __ __ __ __ __ __ whether this class is interesting.

7. Eino Yehudim call Tehillim __ __ __ __ __.

8. Recently, __ __ __ __ __ __ __ __ __ __ has become a popular field.

9. I do not relish having __ __ __ __ __ __ __ __ __ for supper.

10. Most of us had ancestors who were forced to live in a __ __ __ __ __ __.

11. Tisha B'Av is a very __ __ __ __ __ __ day.

12. The spelling words should be written in a __ __ __ __ __ __, not across the page.

13. We __ __ __ __ __ __ __ the recent rise of anti-Semitism hate crimes.

14. As the days grow shorter, __ __ __ __ __ __ draws to a close.

15. We have no __ __ __ __ __ __ openly displaying ourselves as Yiddin when we

    walk in the street.

16. As I get provoked, I remind myself to reply __ __ __ __ __ __ to avoid becoming

    angry.

17. I have a friend who does __ __ __ __ __ __ __ __ for a living.

18. My hand was __ __ __ __ __ __ because I had been writing tefillin for so long.

19. I enjoy listening to his __ __ __ __ __ __ __ __ voice as he prepares the parshah

for leining.

20. Many of the פיוטים __ __ __ __ __ __ well and were therefore easier to read.

Key Concepts
- single tense
- plural tense
- irregular
- vowel
- consonant
- Words ending in y
- present tense
- past tense
- helping verb

When referring to a single noun, surprisingly enough, it is called **singuar**. Even if you are referring to a large group of things or people, if you are treating them as a whole group it is a singular noun. When referring to more than one noun, and not treating them as a collective unit, you need to change to the **plural** form. Most nouns become plural by merely adding **s** to the end of the word. (There are a number of exceptions where **es** is added and other times that the plural form is **irregular**. Irregular means that the word is an exception and does not follow regular rules.) Usually, no change needs to be made to the noun, but there are some exceptions. When the last letter of the noun is **y**, and the letter before the **y** was a consonant, the **y** gets changed to **ie**.

A **vowel** is a sound that is made with the open mouth or throat and works like a נקודה to tell you how to pronounce the other letters. A **consonant** it any letter sound that is not a vowel.

This same rule also applies to nearly all words that end with y when a suffix beginning with a vowel is added to the word – the **y** changes to **ie** (**toy** + **ed** becomes **toyed**, and **baby** + **ed** becomes **babied**[18]). The suffix **ing** is an exception (just like **toy** + **ing** becomes **toying**, **baby** + **ing** becomes **babying**). If the suffix begins with a consonant, no change is made to the **y** (**baby** + **hood** becomes **babyhood**). This pattern regarding suffixes causing changes to the final letter of the base word is similar to the rule you learned in lessons 1 and 2 – if the suffix begins with a vowel it causes the change, but not if it begins with a consonant.

Verbs can be in a number of different forms, called tenses. Some of the easier tenses are past, present, and future. **Past tense** talks about having done the verb in the past. **Present tense** refers to doing the verb now. Future tense means that the verb is going to be done later. Most verbs take the present tense by merely adding an **s** to the verb (**help** becomes **helps**). Most verbs are changed to past tense by adding **ed** to the verb (**help** becomes **helped**). The way to write future tense in English is to use **helping verbs** that show that it will or might be done later. Examples of helping verbs are **might**, **could**, **should**, **will**, **would**, etc.

Lesson Spelling Rule: If the letter before a final **y** is a vowel, do not change the **y** when you add a suffix. If the letter before the final **y** is a consonant, change the **y** to **i** before you add any suffix except **ing**. The **y** never changes before **ing**.

---

18 Even though the suffix added is **ed**, the e is not doubled. **Babied** instead of babieed.

		+ s	+ ed	+ ing
1.	SWAY	SWAYS	SWAYED	SWAYING
2.	CONVEY	CONVEYS	CONVEYED	CONVEYING
3.	DEFRAY	DEFRAYS	DEFRAYED	DEFRAYING
4.	DISMAY	DISMAYS	DISMAYED	DISMAYING
5.	EMPLOY	EMPLOYS	EMPLOYED	EMPLOYING
6.	DECOY	DECOYS	DECOYED	DECOYING
7.	SUBWAY	SUBWAYS		
8.	MEDLEY	MEDLEYS		
9.	ATTORNEY	ATTORNEYS		
10.	EMPLOY	EMPLOYS		
11.	APPLY	APPLIES	APPLIED	APPLYING
12.	DEFY	DEFIES	DEFYED	DEFYING
13.	ENVY	ENVIES	ENVIED	ENVYING
14.	TALLY	TALLIES	TALLIED	TALLYING
15.	MODIFY	MODIFIES	MODIFIED	MODIFYING
16.	CELEBRITY	CELEBRITIES		
17.	CENTURY	CENTURIES		
18.	PENALTY	PENALTIES		
19.	GALLERY	GALLERIES		
20.	AGENCY	AGENCIES		

Pay attention to the spelling words.

1. How many of the words in the first column have a vowel before the final **y**?_____

2. What happens to the **y** when a suffix is added? _____

3. When the letter before the final **y** is a consonant, what happens to the final **y** when

    the suffixes **es** or **ed** is added? _____

4. When **ing** is added to any final **y** word what happens to the **y**?

    _____

> If the letter before a final **y** is a vowel, do not change the **y** when you add a suffix. If the letter before the final **y** is a consonant, change the **y** to **i** before you add any suffix except **ing**. The **y** never changes before **ing**.

Spelling Dictionary

1. **a·gen·cy**   *n.* the work or place of work of any person, firm, authorized to act for another [an insurance *agency*]

2. **ap·ply**   *v.* **–plied, –ply·ing** 1. to put on [to *apply* salve] 2. to make a formal request [to *apply* for a job] 3. to be suitable or relevant [this rule *applies* to everyone]

3. **at·tor·ney**   *n.* any person having the legal power to act for another; esp. a lawyer

4. **ce·leb·ri·ty**   *n.* a famous person

5. **cen·tu·ry**   *n.* any period of 100 years

6. **con·vey**   *v.* **–veyed, –vey·ing** 1. to take from one place to another; transport; carry [the cattle were *conveyed* in trucks to the market] 2. to make known; communicate [writing a note to *convey* his sympathy]

7. **de·coy**   *n.* an artificial bird or animal used to lure game to a place where it can be shot   *–v.* **–coyed, –coy·ing** to lure with false promise

8. **de·fray**   *v.* **–frayed, –fray·ing** to pay (the cost or expenses)

9. **de·fy**   *v.* **–fied, –fy·ing** 1. to resist or oppose boldly or openly [to *defy* the law] 2. to resist completely in a confusing way [the puzzle *defied* solution]

10. **dis·may**   *v.* to make discouraged at the prospect of trouble; fill with alarm   *--n.* a loss of courage when faced with trouble or danger

11. **em·ploy**   *v.* **–ployed, –ploy·ing** 1. to make use of; use [she *employs* skill in her work] 2. to engage the services or labor of for pay; hire

12. **en·vy**   *n.* feeling of discontent and ill will because another has advantages, possessions, etc. that one would like to have   *–v.* **–vied, –vy·ing** to feel envy toward, at, or because of

13. **gal·le·ry**   *n.* a room, building, or establishment for showing or selling art works

14. **med·ley**   *n.* a musical piece made up of tunes or passages from various works

15. **mod·i·fy**   *v.* **–fied, –fy·ing** to change or alter, especially slightly

16. **pe·nal·ty**   *n.* 1. a punishment fixed by law, as for a crime 2. any disadvantage, put on one side in a contest for breaking a rule

17. **pul·ley**   *n.* small wheel with a grooved rim in which a rope or chain runs, as to raise a weight attached at one end by pulling on the other end

18. **sub·way**   *n.* an underground electric railway in some large cities

19. **sway**   *v.* **swayed, –sway·ing** 1. to swing or move from side to side or to and fro [the flowers *swayed* in the breeze] 2. to lean or go to one side; veer [the car *swayed* to the right]

20. **tal·ly**   *n.* an account, reckoning, or score [keep a *tally* of what you spend]   *–v.* **–lied, –ly·ing** to count [usually with *up*] [*tally* up the score]

Practicing the words

A. Writing

The singular form of a noun is usually changed to plural by simply adding **s**. However, when the last letter is **y**, sometimes a slight change needs to be made to the base word. If the letter right before the **y** is a vowel, no change is needed and simply add the **s**. If the letter preceding the **y** is a consonant, then the **y** must be changed to an **i** and **es** must be added.

When a verb is mentioned as if it is taking place right now, that is the present tense. If it will be done later, then you must use the future tense of the verb – usually by adding a helping verb that shows it will be done. To show that the verb already happened, you need to change the present tense to past tense, usually by adding the suffix **ed** to the verb.

Rewrite each sentence. Change the underlined noun to the plural form. Put the underlined verb in its past tense (**ed**) form.

1.   The insurance <u>agency</u> <u>employs</u> many people._____

_____

2.   Mr. Shaw's <u>decoy</u> <u>sways</u> gently on the pond._____

_____

3.   The <u>penalty</u> <u>dismays</u> the hockey player._____

_____

4.   Our art <u>gallery</u> <u>defrays</u> the cost of the exhibit. _____

_____

5.   The <u>subway</u> <u>conveys</u> thousands of commuters._____

_____

6.   Which <u>century</u> in the past <u>defies</u> understanding?_____

_____

7.   The <u>pulley</u> <u>modifies</u> the distribution of weight._____

_____

8.   The other <u>celebrity</u> <u>envies</u> the star of the show._____

_____

9.   The singers of the <u>medley</u> <u>apply</u> new words to old tunes._____

_____

10.   Which firm's <u>attorney</u> <u>tallies</u> the results?_____

_____

B. Limerick

A limerick is a rhymed poem of five lines, about foolishness. The first, second, and last lines end with one rhyming sound. The third and fourth lines end with a different rhyme. Although gibberish is not acceptable, a limerick only has to loosely make sense. It generally states something cute or foolish and is meant to be amusing.

Complete this limerick with five spelling words. The beginning and ending letters are given as clues.

1. The old porch swing gently was s __ __ __ __ __ g;   _____

2. Paul and Max was the swing c __ __ __ __ __ __ __ g.   _____

3. For Max's cookie Paul a __ __ __ __ __ d,   _____

4. But Max firmly d __ __ __ __ d.   _____

5. Paul's evening was truly d __ __ __ __ __ __ __ g.   _____

C. Writing
Some words that end with **f** or **fe** form the plural by changing **f** to **v** and adding **es**[19].
Expand each phrase into a complete sentence using the plural form of the underlined word, which will need to be made plural in this manner. Then circle the spelling word in each sentence.

1. gently swaying <u>leaf</u> –_____

_____

2. defrayed the cost of new library <u>shelf</u> –_____

_____

3. penalties in both <u>half</u> –_____

_____

4. envied the exciting <u>life</u> of hatzoloh members –_____

_____

5. traveled on the subway by <u>themself</u> –_____

_____

6. attorneys who prosecuted the two <u>thief</u> –_____

_____

_____

19 Although this is not a hard and fast rule, generally, it needs to be done when the letter before the **f** is a consonant or the word ends in **fe**.

D. Vowels

Is the letter **y** a consonant or a vowel? The debate continues to rage about this, but generally the rule is that when the **y** is working with another vowel and is beginning the syllable, it is considered a consonant. Think, **yellow** or **yesterday**. But when it follows a consonant and functions as the instruction for pronouncing that syllable, it is treated as a vowel. Think, **syllable** or **sky**.

Lashon Hakodesh also has vowels, called נקודות, but they are distinct from the letters. In תורה שבכתב, there are no vowels, only letters. The נקודות are part of תורה שבעל פה. One analogy that the Rishonim use (it comes from a Kabbalistic Medrash) to describe the relationship between letters and נקודות is that of the body and soul. The נקודות are like the soul of the letters, allowing them to "move" as the word is spoken. The vowel system of Lashon Hakodesh is divided in two systems that work differently with regards to forming syllables.[20] These two systems are called תנועה קטנה and תנועה גדולה. The תנועות גדולות are regular קמץ (not חטף קמץ or קמץ קטן), צירה, (קמץ קטן). The תנועות קטנות are קמץ קטן, פתח, סגול, חיריק מלא, חולם מלאופם. The תנועות קטנות are חיריק חסר, and שורוק.

[There is another group of נקודות that comprise the שוא family. They are שוא נח, שוא נע, חטף קמץ, חטף פתח, and חטף סגול. They are not called תנועות at all, and never form their own syllable. A שוא נח is always part of the syllable before it, and a שוא נע or חטף is always the beginning of the next syllable.]

---

20   One aspect of this distinction is with regards to the שוא that follows the נקודה. If it is a תנועה גדולה, then the שוא is a שוא נע (a moving שוא that is pronounced like the **i** in **if**). If it is a תנועה קלה the שוא will usually be a שוא נח (a silent שוא) where only the letter is pronounced as part of the syllable.

Another distinction is with regards to דגש, the tiny dot that appears in middle of the letters בגדכפת. If they follow a תנועה גדולה they will not have a דגש (think דָבָר), but if they follow תנועה קטנה, they often have a דגש (think שַׁבָּת).

E. Fill in the blanks with the appropriate spelling word.

1. If you shuckel, you __ __ __ __ while davening.

2. I use sentences to __ __ __ __ __ __ the meaning of the words.

3. Moadim Lesimcha helps __ __ __ __ __ __ the cost of making Yom Tov.

4. To the class's __ __ __ __ __ __ , the teacher ended up coming.

5. The gabbai is in the __ __ __ __ __ __ of the Rebbe.

6. To ride the __ __ __ __ __ __ __ , you go underground.

7. You make בורא מיני בשמים over a __ __ __ __ __ __ of spices.

8. You might need an __ __ __ __ __ __ __ __ if you text and drive.

9. A __ __ __ __ __ __ makes it easier to lift.

10. The thief made a __ __ __ __ __ to cover his trail.

11. When you __ __ __ __ __ yourself, you succeed.

12. It is unacceptable to __ __ __ __ the hanhalah's authority.

13. It is very good to __ __ __ __ other people's מעשים טובים.

14. The __ __ __ __ __ of the Chanukah candles without the shamash is 36.

15. Including the shamash will __ __ __ __ __ __ the sum to 44.

16. We had a __ __ __ __ __ __ __ __ __ singer come to our mesibah.

17. We live in the 2K __ __ __ __ __ __ __ , otherwise known as the twenty-first.

18. The __ __ __ __ __ __ __ for writing on the wrong side of the page is being left

    out of the raffle.

19. The Ezras Noshim is a __ __ __ __ __ __ __ overlooking the Bais Medrash.

20. The English word for שליחות is __ __ __ __ __ __ .

Key Concepts
- adjective
- adverb
- noun
- synonym
- antonym
- analogy

A **noun** is a word that is a person, place, or thing. It might be a tangible thing, which means that you can touch it, or an intangible thing, which cannot be touched like an idea. (For example, **hunger**; it is an intangible thing.)

An **adjective** is a word that modifies, limits, or describes a noun. (For example, **worldwide** hunger; it describes where the hunger is.)

An **adverb** is a word that modifies, limits, or describes a verb. That means it tells you about the action or state of being that is the verb. (For example ate **hungrily**; the verb is ate and hungrily tells you about how he ate.)

Words that share similar meanings are **synonyms**. The opposite of a synonym is an **antonym**. It is a pair of words that have meanings that are nearly opposite of each other. An easy mnemonic to help you remember which is which, is that synonym begins with a sound that is similar to similar, which is what it means: a word that is similar. On the other hand, antonym begins with a sound that is similar to anti, which is what it means: a word that is nearly opposite, or anti, the first word.

An **analogy** is a type of comparison between two things that shows a similarity. A more sophisticated analogy draws a comparison between the relationship that one set of pairs has to do with another set of pair.

Lesson Spelling Rule: When you add the suffix **ly** to words that end with **al**, remember that one **l** belongs to the base word, and one **l** belongs to the suffix. Remember to spell the unstressed **a**.

	Adjective			Adverb			Noun
1.	LOCAL	+ LY =	LOCALLY	+ ITY =	LOCALITY
2.	FINAL	+ LY =	FINAL	+ ITY =	FINALITY
3.	LEGAL	+ LY =	LEGAL	+ ITY =	LEGALITY
4.	EQUAL	+ LY =	EQUAL	+ ITY =	EQUALITY
5.	FATAL	+ LY =	FATAL	+ ITY =	FATALITY
6.	ACTUAL	+ LY =	ACTUAL	+ ITY =	ACTUALITY
7.	REAL	+ LY =	REAL	+ ITY =	REALITY
8.	TOTAL	+ LY =	TOTAL	+ ITY =	TOTALITY
9.	MENTAL	+ LY =	MENTAL	+ ITY =	MENTALITY
10.	MORAL	+ LY =	MORAL	+ ITY =	MORALITY
11.	NATIONAL	+ LY =	NATIONAL	+ ITY =	NATIONALITY
12.	PUNCTUAL	+ LY =	PUNCTUAL	+ ITY =	PUNCTUALITY
13.	GENERAL	+ LY =	GENERAL	+ ITY =	GENERALITY
14.	PERSONAL	+ LY =	PERSONAL	+ ITY =	PERSONALITY
15.	INDIVIDUAL	+ LY =	INDIVIDUAL	+ ITY =	INDIVIDUALITY
16.	ORIGINAL	+ LY =	ORIGINAL	+ ITY =	ORIGINALITY
17.	PRACTICAL	+ LY =	PRACTICAL	+ ITY =	PRACTICALITY
18.	FORMAL	+ LY =	FORMAL	+ ITY =	FORMALITY
19.	TECHNICAL	+ LY =	TECHNICAL	+ ITY =	TECHNICALITY
20.	SENTIMENTAL	+ LY =	SENTIMENTAL	+ ITY =	SENTIMENTALITY

Pay attention to the spelling words.

1. All of the adjectives in the first column end with what two letters? _____

2. What two-letter suffix is added to change the adjective to an adverb? _____

3. When the suffix **ly** is added to words that endy with the letter **l**, is one of

   the **l**'s dropped?____

4. What are the last *four* letters of each new adverb?_____

5. Is the unstressed **a** in this ending easy to hear and identify? _____

6. Is the letter **a** easier to hear in the words formed by adding the **ity** suffix?

> When you add the suffix **ly** to words that end with **al**, remember that one l belongs to the base word, and one b belongs to the suffix. Don't drop either of the **l**'s.
> Remember the unstressed **a** by thinking of a related form of the word in which the accent shifts to the **a** (for example, **formally** to **formality)**.

99

Spelling Dictionary

1. **ac·tu·al** — *adj.* 1. presently existing 2. essential
2. **ac·tu·al·i·ty** — *n.* 1. a reality 2. an actual thing or condition; fact
3. **ac·tu·al·ly** — *adv.* as a matter of actual fact; really
4. **e·qual** — *adj.* having the same qualities
5. **e·qual·i·ty** — *n.* state or instance of being equal, esp. of having the same political, economic, and social rights
6. **e·qual·ly** — *adv.* in an equal manner; to an equal degree
7. **fa·tal** — *adj.* 1. fateful; decisive [the *fatal* day arrived] 2. resulting in death 3. having to do with death 4. having dire consequences; bringing ruin;
8. **fa·tal·i·ty** — *n.* 1. something caused by fate 2. a death caused by disaster, as in an accident, war, etc.
9. **fa·tal·ly** — *adv.* with fatal consequences
10. **fi·nal** — *adj.* 1. at the end 2. not to be undone
11. **fi·nal·i·ty** — *n.* the quality or condition of being final, settled, or complete
12. **fi·nal·ly** — *adv.* at the end; in conclusion
13. **for·mal** — *adj.* 1. according to fixed rules, customs, etc. 2. designed for wear at ceremonies, etc. [*formal* dress] 3; refined; befitting royalty or authority
14. **for·mal·i·ty** — *n.* 1. the following of established customs, rules, ceremonies, etc.; propriety 2. a formal or conventional act or requirement; ceremony or form
15. **for·mal·ly** — *adv.* with official authorization; in a formal manner
16. **gen·er·al** — *adj.* 1. of, from, or for the whole or all; not particular or specialized 2. most common; usual [[the *general* spelling of a word] 3. applying to most members; common to the public 4. affecting the entire body   —*n.* any of various military officers ranking above a colonel
17. **gen·er·al·i·ty** — *n.* a statement, expression, etc. that is general or vague rather than definite or with details
18. **gen·er·al·ly** — *adv.* 1. to or by most people; widely [is that fact *generally* known?] 2. in most instances; usually [I *generally* go straight home] 3. in a general way; without going into details [speaking *generally,* I'd agree]
19. **in·di·vid·u·al** — *adj.* 1. separate from others 2. concerning a specific person
20. **in·di·vid·u·al·i·ty** — *n.* the qualities that set one person or thing apart from others; individual character
21. **in·di·vid·u·al·ly** — *adv.* one at a time; separately
22. **le·gal** — *adj.* of, based on, or authorized by law [*legal* studies]
23. **le·gal·i·ty** — *n.* quality, instance, or condition of being legal or lawful
24. **le·gal·ly** — *adv.* 1. by law 2. conforming to the law 3. in a legal manner
25. **lo·cal** — *adj.* related or pertaining to a specific area
26. **lo·cal·i·ty** — *n.* a place; district

27. **lo·cal·ly**   *adv.* within a given area or areas [the damage done by a tornado *locally*]
28. **men·tal**   *adj.* 1. involving the mind   2. of or for the mind
29. **men·tal·i·ty**   *n.* mental capacity, power or activity; mind
30. **men·tal·ly**   *adv.* in the mind
31. **mor·al**   *adj.* 1. related to, dealing with, or capable of distinguishing between right and wrong in conduct [a *moral* question]   2. concerned with principles or standards of behavior
32. **mor·al·i·ty**   *n.* moral quality or character; rightness or wrongness, as of an action
33. **mor·al·ly**   *adv.* with respect to moral principles; in a moral manner
34. **na·tion·al**   *adj.* related or belonging to a country or the country [*national* anthem]
35. **na·tion·al·i·ty**   *n.* the status of belonging to a particular nation by birth or nationalization
36. **na·tion·al·ly**   *adv.* with regard to the nation as a whole; extending throughout a nation
37. **o·rig·i·nal**   *adj.* 1. fresh; new; novel [an *original* idea]   2. first   3. not copied
38. **o·rig·i·nal·i·ty**   *n.* 1. the quality of being original   2. the ability to be original, inventive, or creative
39. **o·rig·i·nal·ly**   *adv.* 1. before now; with reference to the beginning   2. in an original manner
40. **per·son·al**   *adj.* 1. concerning or pertaining to a specific individual   2. private
41. **per·so·nal·i·ty**   *n.* 1. all the special qualities of a person which make him different from other people   2. a person, esp. a famous person
42. **per·son·al·ly**   *adv.* 1. without the help of others; in person [to attend to a matter *personally*]   2. in one's own opinion   3. as though directed at oneself [to take a remark *personally*]
43. **prac·ti·cal**   *adj.* 1. usable; workable; useful and sensible [*practical* proposals]   2. concerned with actual use or practice   3. being actual nearly in every respect [a *practical* failure]
44. **prac·ti·cal·i·ty**   *n.* the quality of being concerned with actual use rather than theoretial possibility
45. **prac·ti·cal·ly**   *adv.* 1. in a practical way   2. in effect; really; virtually [*practically* a dictator]   3. [Colloq.[21]] nearly [we're *practically* home]
46. **punc·tu·al**   *adj.* acting or arriving exactly at the appointed time; on time; prompt
47. **punc·tu·a·li·ty**   *n.* the quality or habit of adhering to an appointed time
48. **punc·tu·al·ly**   *adv.* at the expected or proper time
49. **real**   *adj.* 1. occuring in fact   2. essential

---

21 Colloq. stands for colloquialism. It is means informal speech.

50. **re·al·i·ty**   *n.* the quality or fact of being real **–in reality** in fact; actually

51. **re·al·ly**   *adv.* 1. in reality; in fact   2. truly or genuine [*really* hot]

52. **sen·ti·men·tal**   *adj.* 1. having or showing tender or gentle feelngs, often in a foolish way [a *sentimental* song]   2. of or resulting from sentiment [to save a picture for *sentimental* feelings]   3. given to sentiment; overly emotional

53. **sen·ti·men·tal·i·ty**   *n.* the quality or condition of being sentimental, especially in a foolish way

54. **sen·ti·men·tal·ly**   *adv.* in a sentimental manner

55. **tech·ni·cal**   *adj.* 1. of or used in a specific science, art craft, etc. [*technical* terms]   2. relating to technique; showing skill   3. concerned with machinery   4. strictly adhering to rules

56. **tech·ni·cal·i·ty**   *n.* 1. a technical point, term, method, etc.   2. a minute, formal point or detail

57. **tech·ni·cal·ly**   *adv.* with regards to techniques; according to the exact meaning

58. **to·tal**   *adj.* 1. making up the (or a) whole; entire [the *total* amount is ten dollars]   2. complete; utter [a *total* loss]

59. **to·tal·ity**   *n.* 1. the fact or condition of being total   2. the total amount or sum

60. **to·tal·ly**   *adv.* completely; entirely

Practicing the words

A. Use the adjective, adverb, and noun forms of a spelling word to complete each set of phrases. Remember that an adjective modifies a noun and an adverb modifies a verb. If the phrase contains no verb, then it can only be an adjective or a noun. If the phrase contains a verb and a noun, there's a good chances are that the spelling word will be an adjective or adverb (although sometimes its another noun).

1. _____ habits

take a remark _____

a public _____

2. demand _____ time

_____ difficult options

racial _____

3. a _____ song

looked at old photos _____

a story full of _____

4. a _____ invitation

were _____ introduced

a mere _____

5. the _____ moments of the game

_____ admitted she was wrong

spoke with _____

6. an _____ idea

_____ came from Toronto

an award for _____

7. _____ time

_____ grown honey

moving to a new _____

8. a _____ document

_____ valid

a mere _____

9. a _____ accident

a _____ important decision

the _____ of war

10. _____ fact

we _____ won

it became an _____

11. _____ time

_____ neat idea

turn your dream into _____

12. the _____ was 85

_____ prepared

the _____ of all the parts

103

B. Proofreading
Cross out the misspelled word or words in each sentence and rewrite them correctly.
1. The judge finaly dismissed the case because of a legal tecnicality._____

_____

2. Yanina's punctuality and individuallity are realy appreciated by everyone. _____

_____

3. The senator's generallity about the economy was technicaly incorrect. _____

_____

4. Originaly, all our vegetables were grown localy. _____

_____

5. Practicaly every nationalety was represented at the conference. _____

_____

6. I personaly think that Chana's answer had a note of finallity about it. _____

_____

7. Actualy, we were never formalley introduced. _____

_____

8. Generaly, the chores are equaley divided among the campers. _____

_____

C. Synonyms and antonyms

SYNONYMS are words that have almost the same meaning

ANTONYMS are words that have the opposite meaning

A. Write the adverb (**ly**) form of a spelling word that is a synonym (**S**) or an antonym (**A**) for each word in the first column. Write a noun (**ity**) form of a spelling word that is a synonym or antonym for each word in the second column.

1. completely (**S**)	_____	1. site (**S**)	_____
2. physically (**A**)	_____	2. death (**S**)	_____
3. lastly (**S**)	_____	3. inequality (**A**)	_____
4. promptly (**S**)	_____	4. entirety (**S**)	_____
5. locally (**A**)	_____	5. unreality (**A**)	_____
6. lawfully (**S**)	_____	6. lawfulness (**S**)	_____
7. unitedly (**A**)	_____	7. informality (**A**)	_____
8. really (**S**)	_____	8. intelligence (**S**)	_____
9. unethically (**A**)	_____	9. immorality (**A**)	_____
10. lethally (**S**)	_____	10. reality (**S**)	_____

D. Analogies

An **analogy** is a type of comparison between two things that shows a similarity. A more sophisticated analogy draws a comparison between the relationship that one set of pairs has to do with another set of pairs.

Complete each analogy with a spelling word. Use the form of the spelling word that is the same part of speech as the word with which it is paired: use a noun with a noun an adjective with an adjective.

1. **oak** is to **tree** as **specifically** is to _____

2. **body** is to **mind** as **physically** is to _____

3. **tall** is to **short** as **tardiness** is to _____

4. **Atlantic** is to **ocean** as **Italian** is to _____

5. **jeans** is to **tuxedo** as **casualness** is to _____

6. **some** is to **all** as **partially** is to _____

7. **sport** is to **tennis** as **emotion** is to _____

8. **first** is to **last** as **originally** is to _____

E. Fill in the blanks with the appropriate spelling word.

1. Our Cheder is __ __ __ __ __ __ __ known to be one of the best mosdos.

2. We use punctuation marks to show __ __ __ __ __ __ __ __ to our statements.

3. Serving liquor to minors is not __ __ __ __ __ __ __ permitted.

4. Racial __ __ __ __ __ __ __ __ is not necessarily a Torah ideal.

5. President Lincoln was __ __ __ __ __ __ __ shot by the assassin.

6. In __ __ __ __ __ __ __ __ __, it seems Congress is headed to Impeaching the president.

7. It is __ __ __ __ __ __ going to happen.

8. The __ __ __ __ __ __ __ __ of Yiddin comprise 600,000 neshamos.

9. Most of our students are __ __ __ __ __ __ __ __ gifted.

10. The __ __ __ __ __ __ __ __ of the דור המבול was in terrible condition.

11. Jared Kushner is a __ __ __ __ __ __ __ __ __ __ renowned Jew.

12. Our class can improve our __ __ __ __ __ __ __ __ __ __ __.

13. __ __ __ __ __ __ __ __ __ speaking, this class is well-behaved.

14. His work-driven __ __ __ __ __ __ __ __ __ __ helps him achieve.

15. Every student must take the test __ __ __ __ __ __ __ __ __ __ __ __.

16. Many boys surprised me with their __ __ __ __ __ __ __ __ __ __ __ when writing their essay.

17. The 'a' sound is __ __ __ __ __ __ __ __ __ __ __ not pronounced when it comes between c and l.

18. Many times we say 'I'm sorry' merely as a __ __ __ __ __ __ __ __, without meaning it.

19. An incomplete stop at the stop sign is __ __ __ __ __ __ __ __ __ __ a violation of the law.

20. Too much __ __ __ __ __ __ __ __ __ __ __ __ __ during a speech can make the audience uncomfortable.

Key Concepts
- changing verbs to adjectives
- changing verb to nouns
- changing adjectives to adverbs
- synonyms
- synonymy

Many verbs can be changed to an adjective by adding the suffix **able/ible**. When added to the verb, the adjective means "able to be or do the verb."

Verbs can also be changed to nouns by adding the suffix **ance/ence**. Remember that nouns can be intangible[22] things like ideas, and this noun will mean "the idea of the verb."

Another way to form an adjective is to add the suffix **ant/ent**, which will mean "that which has or shows the base or root."

Many adjectives can be changed to adverbs by adding the suffix **ly**, which will mean "in the manner of the adjective."

Synonyms are words that have similar meanings. A **synonymy** is a section of the dictionary that lists synonyms of the word and might contain short words or phrases to explain differences between their meanings

Lesson Spelling Rule: The suffixes **able** and **ance** are more commonly added to complete words than to roots. The suffixes **ible**, **ence**, and **ent** are more commonly added to roots than to complete words.

The suffix **able/ible** forms adjectives meaning **able to be**.

The suffixe **ance/ence** is a noun ending that converts a verb to a noun.

The suffix **ant/ent** can form adjectives meaning **that which has or shows**.

Prefixes used in this lesson, together with their meanings:
- sus[23]- means under
- ex- means beyond, out of, thoroughly, former, previous
- im- means no, not, without
- in- means no, not, without
- pro- means before in place or time; forward or ahead
- pre- means before in time, place or rank
- com[24]- means with, together, or all together; very or very much
- per- means throughout; thoroughly
- ad- means toward

Suffixes used in this lesson, together with their meanings:
- -ant/ent (that has or shows)
- -ance/ence (act of, state of being)
- -able/ible (able to be or do)
- -ly (in the manner of)

---

22 Intangible means that cannot be touched.
23 In a later lesson you will learn that it really is a form of the prefix sub, meaning under.
24 In a later lesson you will learn that it really is a form of the prefix con, meaning all together.

Base Word		Suffix			Suffix		
1. depend	+	able	= dependable	+	ly	=	dependably
2. accept	+	able	= acceptable	+	ly	=	acceptably
3. approach	+	able	= approachable				
4. obtain	+	able	= obtainable				
5. detect	+	able	= detectable				
6. clear	+	ance	= clearance				
7. resemble	+	ance	= resemblance				
8. ignore	+	ance	= ignorance	+	ant	=	ignorant
9. comply	+	ance	= compliance	+	ant	=	compliant
10. ally	+	ance	= alliance				

Prefix		Root		Suffix			Suffix		
1. com	+	pat	+	ible	= compatible	+	ly	=	compatibly
2. sus	+	cept	+	ible	= susceptible				
3. per	+	miss	+	ible	= permissible	+	ly	=	permissibly
4. im	+	poss	+	ible	= impossible	+	ly	=	impossibly
5. in	+	cred	+	ible	= incredible	+	ly	=	incredibly
6. ex	+	peri			= experience				
7. in	+	gredi				+	ent	=	ingredient
8. pro	+	min	+	ence	= prominence	+	ent	=	prominent
9. per	+	man	+	ence	= permanence	+	ent	=	permanent
10. ad	+	jac				+	ent	=	adjacent

Pay attention to the spelling words.

1. What four suffixes are added to complete words? _____
   _____ _____ _____
2. What happens to the final silent **e** words when a suffix beginning with a vowel is added to these words?
   _____
3. What happens to the words that end with a **y** preceded by a consonant? _____
4. Are the suffixes **ible**, **ence**, and **ent** added to complete words or to roots? _____
5. Which suffix corresponding to **ent** is added to complete words? _____

> The suffixes **able** and **ance** are more commonly added to complete words than to roots. The suffixes **ible**, **ence**, and **ent** are more commonly added to roots than to complete words.
> The suffix **able/ible** forms adjectives meaning **able to be**.
> The suffixe **ance/ence** is a noun ending that converts a verb to a noun.
> The suffix **ant/ent** can form adjectives meaning **that which has or shows**.

1. **ac·cept** — *v.* **–cep·ted, –cept·ing** to take; receive willingly
2. **ac·cept·a·ble** — *adj.* worth accepting; satisfactory, or sometimes, merely adequate
3. **ac·cept·ab·ly** — *adv.* in an acceptable (but not outstanding) manner
4. **ad·ja·cent** — *adj.* near or close (*to* something); adjoining
5. **al·li·ance** — *n.* a close association for a common goal, as of nations, parties, etc.
6. **al·ly** — *n.* 1. a friendly nation 2. an associate who provides assistance or cooperation —*v.* **–lied, –ly·ing** become an ally or associate, as by a treaty or marriage
7. **ap·proach** — *v.* **–proached, –proach·ing** 1. move towards 2. come near or verge on —*n.* 1. ideas or actions intended to deal with a problem or situation 2. the act of drawing closer to something
8. **ap·proach·a·ble** — *adj.* capable of being approached; accessible
9. **clear** — *adj.* 1. free from confusion or doubt 2. affording free passage or view —*v.* **cleared, clear·ing** 1. remove 2. rid of obstructions 3. grant authorization or clearance for
10. **clear·ance** — *n.* 1. an act or process of clearing: as (a) a sale to clear out stock (b) authorization 2. the clear space between things
11. **com·pat·i·ble** — *adj.* capable of living together in harmony or getting along well together
12. **com·pat·ib·ly** — *adv.* in a compatible manner
13. **com·pli·ance** — *n.* a complying by giving in to a request, demand, etc. or following a rule or requirement
14. **com·pli·ant** — *adj.* inclined to comply
15. **com·ply** — *v.* **–plied, –ply·ing** act in accordance with someone's rules, commands, or wishes
16. **de·pend** — *v.* **–pen·ded, –pend·ing** 1. have faith or confidence in 2. be determined by conditions or circumstances 3. hang
17. **de·pend·a·ble** — *adj.* that can be depended on
    SYN[25]. – **dependable** refers to a person or thing that can be depended on as in an emergency and often suggest personal loyalty, levelheadedness, or steadiness [she is a *dependable* friend]; **reliable** is used of a person or thing that can be counted upon to do what is expected or required [his *reliable* assistant]; **trusty** applies to a person or thing that has in the past always been trustworthy or dependable [his *trusty* horse]
18. **de·pend·ab·ly** — *adv.* in a faithful manner
19. **de·tect** — *v.* **–tec·ted, –tect·ing** to discover (something hidden or not easily noticed) [to *detect* a slight flaw in an argument]
20. **de·tect·a·ble** — *adj.* 1. capable of being detected 2. easily seen or noticed
21. **ex·per·i·ence** — *n.* the act of living through an event or events [*experience* teaches us much]
22. **ig·nor·ance** — *n.* lack of knowledge
23. **ig·nor·ant** — *adj.* 1. uneducated; lacking knowledge 2. unaware because of a lack of relevant information or knowledge

---

25 Syn. stands for synonymy. It is a list of synonyms found at the end of the entry in some words in a dictionary.

24. **ig·nore**   *v.* **–nored, –nor·ing** 1. refuse to acknowledge   2. fail to notice   3. be ignorant of

25. **im·pos·si·ble**   *adj.* not possible; not capable of being or happening

26. **im·pos·sib·ly**   *adv.* to a degree not possible of achieving

27. **in·cred·i·ble**   *adj.* 1. not credible; unbelievable [an *incredible* story]   2. so great, unusual, etc. as to seem impossible [*incredible* speed]

28. **in·cred·ib·ly**   *adv.* 1. not easy to believe   2. exceedingly; extremely

29. **in·gred·i·ent** *n.* any of the things that a mixture is made of [sugar is a basic *ingredient* of candy]

30. **ob·tain**   *v.* **–tained, –tain·ing** to get possession of by effort

31. **ob·tain·a·ble**   *adj.* capable of being obtained

32. **per·ma·nence**   *n.* the idea of being able to exist for an indefinite duration

33. **per·ma·nent**   *adj.* lasting, or intended to last indefinitely or for a long time

34. **per·miss·i·ble**   *adj.* that can be permitted; allowable

35. **per·miss·ib·ly**   *adv.* in a permissible manner

36. **pro·mi·nence**   *n.* 1. the state of being prominent; widely known or eminent   2. relative importance   3. something that bulges out or protrudes from its surroundings

37. **pro·mi·nent**   *adj.* 1. noticeable at once; conspicuous [a bird with *prominent* markings]   2. widely and favorably known [a *prominent* artist]
SYN. –**prominent** refers to that which stands out from or as from its background or setting [a *prominent* nose; a *prominent* author]; **noticeable** is applied to that which is likely to be noticed or worth noticing [a *noticeable* improvement]; **remarkable** applies to that which is noticeable because it is unusual or exceptional [*remarkable* features; *remarkable* strength]; **striking** is used of something so out of the ordinary that it leaves a sharp impression on the mind [a *striking* contrast; a *striking* design]

38. **re·sem·blance**   *n.* a point, degree, or sort of likeness
SYN. –**resemblance** usually implies being alike in a superficial way or only seeming alike, as in looks [the *resemblance* between a diamond and a zircon]; **likeness** implies being closely alike in appearance, qualities, nature, etc. [her remarkable *likeness* to her brother]; **similarity** suggest a being alike only in a certain way or to some extent [your problem bears a certain *similarity* to mine]

39. **re·sem·ble**   *v.* **–bled, –bl·ing** appear like; be similar or bear a likeness to

40. **sus·cep·ti·ble**   *adj.* easily affected emotionally; having sensitive feelings
–**susceptible to** easily influenced by or affected with

Practicing the words

A. Finish each incomplete spelling word with the correct ending. Write the complete words after the sentence and indicate which part of speech it is by writing the abbreviation next to each word.

1.   The resembl____ between the sisters was incred____. _____

2.   The ambassadors hoped for a perman____ alli____ between the two compat____ countries.

      _____

3.   Clear____ for that project was not immediately obtain____.

      _____

4.   This ingredi____ is easily detect____. _____

5.   Compli____ with that difficult rule was nearly imposs____. _____

6.   His ignor____ of the important issues makes discussion almost imposs____.

      _____

7.   Your paper on your camping experi____ is not accept____.

      _____

B.

Find the spelling words that are needed to complete the story.

     Charley's family lived in an old house that was ___1___ to a small forest. His house was ___2___ only by walking through the forest. However, in the hot, dry summer months, the forest was ___3___ to fires. Fire marshals had posted signs in ___4___ places to warn people of the danger. Campfires were not ___5___ in the summer.

     One August day, Charley and his dog Fido were on their way home. Suddenly, the smell of smoke was clearly ___6___. Charley assumed that some picnickers were not in ___7___ with the law. Gradually, the smell grew stronger. All at once, Charley and Fido seemed surrounded by an amazing, ___8___ wall of smoke. Fido, who was usually ___9___ in an emergency, started to run away. Charley called her, but she was soon out of sight. Charley froze and didn't know which way to go. Then Fido reappeared and motioned for Charley to follow. She had found a way out! Together, they escaped, but Charley knew he would never forget his frightening ___10___.

7. _____

8. _____

9. _____

10. _____

11. _____

12. _____

13. _____

14. _____

15. _____

16. _____

C. Synonym

A synonymy is a special section at the end of some word entries in a dictionary. It contains a list of synonyms for the entry word. Short phrases or sentences may be included to show the slight differences between the word meanings.

Look up dependable, resemblance, and prominent in your spelling dictionary. Read the synonymy at the end of each entry. Write the synonyms for each word.

dependable _____ _____

prominent _____ _____

resemblance _____ _____ _____

Now complete each sentence with the entry word or synonym that best fits the meaning.

1. The knight rode into battle on his _____ horse.

2. My pony has _____ strength for her size.

3. Leora drew a _____ of her father.

4. We listened to a reading by a _____ poet.

5. Did you notice the _____ between the cousins' faces?

6. Our doctor is always _____ in an emergency.

7. The performer wore a _____ Purim costume.

8. There is a _____ in the weather between the two states.

9. The store owner has a _____ manager who keeps the shop running.

10. There was a _____ drop in attendance at today's game.

D. Some **able** adjectives can be changed to adverbs by switching the final **e** for a **y**. Complete each phrase by writing the adverb form of the underlined spelling word.

1. acceptable dress   dressed _____

2. compatible playmates   played _____

3. dependable behavior   behaved _____

4. impossible task   _____ difficult

5. incredible strength   _____ strong

Now write a complete sentence using the new phrase.

1._____

_____

2._____

_____

3._____

_____

4._____

_____

5._____

_____

E. Fill in the blanks with the appropriate spelling word.

1. This is a class of __ __ __ __ __ __ __ __ __ young adults.

2. It is __ __ __ __ __ __ __ __ __ __ to write in colored pens in this class.

3. The principal is very __ __ __ __ __ __ __ __ __ __ __ __.

4. A great mark is __ __ __ __ __ __ __ __ __ __ when you pay attention.

5. Your effort is often __ __ __ __ __ __ __ __ __ __ in your work.

6. People are __ __ __ __ __ __ __ __ __ __ when they get along together.

7. If you are __ __ __ __ __ __ __ __ __ __ __ to colds, wear a scarf.

8. It is __ __ __ __ __ __ __ __ __ __ if it complies with the rules.

9. It is __ __ __ __ __ __ __ __ __ __ to entirely eradicate all germs.

10. The __ __ __ __ __ __ __ __ __ Dreidel of Feitel Van Zeidel used to be my favorite.

11. After the season, old styles go on __ __ __ __ __ __ __ __ __ sales.

12. Yaakov Avinu bore no __ __ __ __ __ __ __ __ __ __ __ to Eisav.

13. __ __ __ __ __ __ __ __ __ of the law is no excuse.

14. It is permissible if it is in __ __ __ __ __ __ __ __ __ __ with the regulations.

15. Eisav tried an __ __ __ __ __ __ __ __ with Yishmael to overcome Yaakov Avinu.

16. I have some __ __ __ __ __ __ __ __ __ with using good grammar.

17. Perseverance is one __ __ __ __ __ __ __ __ __ __ of success.

18. A __ __ __ __ __ __ __ __ __ feature is very noticeable.

19. Repeating a good practice makes a __ __ __ __ __ __ __ __ __ good habit.

20. The Ezras Noshim is __ __ __ __ __ __ __ __ to the Bais Medrash.

Key Concepts
- preposition
- prefix
- syllables

A **preposition** is a type of word that is placed before a word to show that word's relation to another word in the sentence. It is placed in position before (pre) the word and it tells about the relationship of the following word to the part that came earlier. Some examples of preposition words are between, through, beside, from, to, at, etc.

A prefix can often carry the meaning of a preposition before the rest of the word. It comes before the rest of the word and can tell you about the relationship of the rest of the word to the other parts of the sentence. Understanding the meanings of prefixes can help better remember the meanings of words and can help you discover the meaning of new words better.

A **syllable** is a word part that has a single vowel sound. It might have a number of vowels (**boat**) or not even a single vowel (dan**g**ling). The key is that it is pronounced as a distinct part of the word separate from the other parts – usually with a separate motion of your mouth. A hint to distinguish the different syllables is to pay attention to your chin as you clearly pronounce the word. Each distinct movement of your chin marks a separate syllable. Sometimes an entire words is a single syllable. This is even true of long words such as **brought**.

Lesson Spelling Rule: A prefix often carries the meaning of a preposition before the word.

Prefixes used in this lesson, together with their meanings:
- inter- means between
- para- means alongside
- per- means throughout; thoroughly
- ab- means down or away from
- de- means under or away from

1. INTERMISSION
2. INTERVIEW
3. INTERSTATE
4. INTERPRETER
5. INTERCEPTION
6. INTERRUPT
7. INTERNATIONAL
8. PARAMEDIC
9. PARALLEL
10. PARAPHRASE
11. PERENNIAL
12. PERCOLATE
13. PERFORATED
14. PERPETUAL
15. PERSEVERANCE
16. ABDICATE
17. ABSENCE
18. DESTRUCTION
19. DEPRIVED
20. DEPLETED

Pay attention to the spelling words.

1. The prefix inter means "between." What word refers to events that occur between nations? _____

2. The prefix para means "beside." What word refers to a person who is not a doctor, but who works alongside of or assists medical people?

   _____

3. The prefix per means "through" or "throughout." What word refers to flowers that bloom throughout the year? _____

4. What two prefixes mean "down from" or "away from"?

   _____

> A prefix often carries the meaning of a preposition before a word to show you the relationship of the word with regards to time and place.

Spelling Dictionary

1. **ab·di·cate**   *v.* **–cat·ed, –cat·ing** to give up formally (a high office, etc.)
2. **ab·sence**   *n.* 1. the state of being away   2. the fact of being without; lack [in the *absence* of proof]
3. **con·tra·dic·tion**   *n.* a statement in opposition to another; denial
4. **de·plete**   *v.* **–plet·ed, –plet·ing** to make less by gradually using up (funds, energy, etc.)
5. **de·prive**   *v.* **–prived, –priv·ing** to keep from having, using, or enjoying [*deprived* of the comforts of life by poverty]
6. **de·struc·tion**   *n.* a destroying or being destroyed; ruin [the earthquake caused much *destruction*]
7. **e·dict**   *n.* an official public order or law put forth by a ruler or other authority; decree
8. **in·de·struct·i·ble** *adj.* that cannot be destroyed
9. **in·struc·tion**   *n.* a message describing how something is to be done; direction [*instructions* for a test]
10. **in·ter·cept**   *v.* **–cept·ed, –cept·ing** to seize, stop, or interrupt on the way; cut off [to *intercept* a message]
11. **in·ter·cep·tion**   *n.* 1. the act of intercepting; preventing something from proceeding or arriving   2. (American football) the act of catching a football by a player on the opposing team
12. **in·ter·mis·sion**   *n.* an interval of time between periods of activity; pause, as between acts of a play
13. **in·ter·na·tion·al**   *adj.* between or among nations [an *international* treaty]
14. **in·ter·pre·ter**   *n.* a person whose work is translating things said in another language
15. **in·ter·rupt**   *v.* **–rupt·ed, –rupt·ing** 1. to break into (a discussion, etc.) 2. to break in upon (a person) while he or she is speaking, working, etc.
16. **in·ter·state**   *adj.* between or among states of the federal government [*interstate* commerce]
17. **in·ter·view**   *n.* 1. a meeting of people face to face to talk about something [an *interview* about a job] 2. a meeting in which a person is asked about his or her opinions, activities, etc., as by a reporter   *–v.* **–viewed, –view·ing** 1. to go to an interview in the hope of being hired   2. to conduct an interview
18. **pa·ral·lel**   *adj.* extending in the same direction and always at the same distance apart, so as to never meet
19. **pa·ra·med·ic**   *n.* person who assists a doctor, such as a midwife, aide, or laboratory technician
20. **pa·ra·phrase**   *n.* a putting of something spoken or written into different words having the same meaning; rewording for the purpose of clarification   *–v.* express the same message in different words

21. **per·co·late**   *v.* **–lat·ed, –lat·ing** 1. to pass (a liquid) gradually through a filter   2. to brew (coffee)
22. **per·en·ni·al**   *adj.* 1. lasting or active throughout the whole year   2. becoming active again and again; perpetual [a *perennial* problem]   3. having a life cycle of more than two years: said of plants
23. **per·for·ate**   *v.* **–at·ed, –at·ing** to make a hole or holes through, as by punching or boring, often in a pattern
24. **per·pet·u·al**   *adj.* lasting forever or for an indefinitely long time
25. **per·se·ver·ance**   *n.* persistence; steadfastness; continued, patient effort
26. **re·con·struct**   *v.* **–struc·ted, –struct·ing** to build up again, make over
27. **struc·ture**   *n.* 1. something built or constructed, as a building or dam   2. the arrangement of all the parts of a whole
28. **ver·dict**   *n.* 1. (law) the decision reached by a jury at the end of a trial   2. any decision or judgment

Practicing the words

A. Write the spelling word that matches each definition. Then circle the word in the definition that gives the meaning of the prefix. Next, indicate what part of speech it is by writing the abbreviation next to it..

1. a time of being away _____

2. punched through _____

3. between states _____

4. a tearing down _____

5. continued effort through difficulty _____

6. a coming between to stop or cut off _____

7. two or more things beside each other at an equal distance _____

8. a person who translates between languages _____

9. time in between _____

10. boil a liquid through _____

11. reword "beside" the original _____

12. to have had things taken away from _____

13. a lasting throughout time _____

14. a conversation between people _____

15. step down from a high office _____

16. to rudely break in between _____

B. Make spelling words from these sets of words. First cross out one letter in each word. Then write the remaining letters together to form a spelling word. The first one has been done for you.

intern + ace + potion =   interception

part + call + gel =   _____

perform + hated =   _____

pier + pets + dual =   _____

cab + dice + mate =   _____

winter + amiss + lion =   _____

interns + ration + gal =   _____

cab + sent + ace =   _____

ode + prim + vied =   _____

spar + came + dice =   _____

perk + severe + lance =   _____

perch + old + rate =   _____

deep + lent + red =   _____

pat + graph + raise =   _____

C. A syllable is a portion of a word that has a single vowel sound. It might have no vowels or might have numerous vowels. The vowels might be written together or might be separated by consonants. All the letters that are pronounced with the same vowel SOUND make up the syllable. A hint to remember it is to feel your face change as you clearly enunciate the word. As your face changes to form a new sound segment of the word, that indicates to you that you have completed the first syllable and are beginning a new one. Find a spelling word to complete each sentence. Then write the words broken up according to its syllables. Separate each syllable with a hyphen or a line.

1. Overspending has _____ the treasury.

2. The countries signed an _____ agreement.

3. A nurse and a _____ assisted the doctor.

4. Will you _____ the coffee?

5. The rose is a _____ plant.

6. Draw two _____ lines.

7. We need an _____ for the foreign visitor.

8. The truck has an _____ route.

9. The reporter's _____ was on Kol Beramah.

10. The king had to _____ his throne.

11. The play's _____ is after Act I.

12. The paper is _____ for easy tearing.

D. In לשון הקודש a syllable is called either a יתד or a תנועה. In very many of the פיוטים and שירים from the Spanish and African Rishonim, the basis of the verses were written in a format based on these syllables. There is a slight difference between syllables in לשון הקודש and English. In לשון הקודש, the sound of שוא is not a separate syllable, even though it is pronounced with a different movement of the jaw.

A יתד is a syllable that begins with a שוא נא or its assistants (חטף קמץ, חטף פתח, חטף סגול) and continues with the next נקודה. It continues until the following נקודה, which begins the next syllable.

A תנועה is a syllable that begins with a true נקודה on the letter that begins the syllable. It might just be that letter, or up to three letters, all the letters that are pronounced with that נקודה. A שוא cannot begin a תנועה. If it is a שוא נח, it might end the תנועה if the following letter has a new נקודה or a שוא נע; or the תנועה will continue if the following letter is also a שוא נח. [There are two types of שוא נח – one is pronounced and is called נח נראה (visible), the other is not pronounced and is called נח נסתר (hidden). In the word בראשית, the ת is called a נח נראה because its sound is pronounced, but the א and י are נח נסתר because their sounds are not pronounced.]

For example, in the song for Shabbos day, דרור יקרא, the pattern is יתד ושני תנועות. The first stanza of the song is דרור יק·רא לבן עם בת וין·צר·כם כמו ב·בת נעים שמ·כם ולא יוש·בת שבו ונו·חו ביום ש·בת. The יתד"s have been underlined and bolded. Syllables in a single word have been separated with the dot.

On the next page you have the beginning of the Baal Hamaor's introduction to His Sefer Hamaor on the Rif. It is printed in the Vilna Shas right before the Rif on Maseches Brachos. The parts that might have contained Shaimos have been greyed out. As it states in the beginning of the section that is visible, each verse is comprised of two stanzas, both of which contain a יתד followed by 2 תנועות, another יתד followed by 2 תנועות, a יתד and a single תנועה.

Incredibly, the Baal Hamaor is one of the most difficult Rishonim to understand, yet he writes at the top that he authored it when he was under twenty years old!

כשהוחל החבור הזה היה מחברו בן תשע עשרה שנה ופתח בו בבתים האלה :

... דִּי תושבחתא ... לְדִילַהּ . וּגְבוּרְתָּא .

וכתב על זה אביו החכם רבי יצחק הלוי זל בר זרחיה זל :

שיר לרבינו זרחיה הלוי זל מרובע ופשוט

closing stanza   *opening stanza*   שני תנועות   comprised

שיר מרכב מיתר בית ויתד ובית ויתד ותנועה בדלת וכן בסוגר

קָנְתָה סֵפֶר כְּמוֹ צֹהַר תְּקוּמוֹ . וְכַנֵּר אֶל נְתִיבָתְךָ תְּשִׂימוֹ .
לְיִצְהָרִי זְרַחְיָה בְּמִגְבָּל . יְרָחִי חִבְּרוּ לָנֶּם הֲרִימוֹ .
לְזֹאת מָאוֹר שְׁמוֹ קָרָא לְאוֹת בְּ . עֲבוּר הַזְכִּיר שְׁמוֹ נֶשֶׁם קְקוֹמוֹ .

E. Build a word pyramid by following the code. Use the spelling dictionary to find four pyramid words that match the definitions.

The root **dic** means "to say or proclaim."

11. a decision proclaimed at the end of a trial_____

12. to say that one gives something up_____

13. an official order or proclamation

    _____

14. the opposite of something said

    _____

					D	I	C				
				5	D	I	C	11			
		12	5	10	D	I	C	11			
			1	2	D	I	C	1	11	5	
					D	I	C	11	1	11	5	4
		9	10	5	D	I	C	11	6	8	7
3	8	7	11	10	1	D	I	C	11	6	8	7

A	B	C	D	E	I	N	O	P	R	T	V
1	2	3	4	5	6	7	8	9	10	11	12

F. Build another word pyramid. Find the four pyramid words that match the definitions. The root **struct** means "build."

1. directions on how to "build" something

    _____

2. rebuilt

    _____

3. not able to be destroyed or "unbuilt"

    _____

4. building or construction

    _____

			S	T	R	U	C	T			
			S	T	R	U	C	T	11	9	4
	3	4	S	T	R	U	C	T	5	8	7
	5	7	S	T	R	U	C	T	5	8	7	10
	8	1	S	T	R	U	C	T	5	8	7
9	4	2	8	7	S	T	R	U	C	T	4	3
5	7	3	4	S	T	R	U	C	T	5	1	6	4

B	C	D	E	I	L	N	O	R	S	U
1	2	3	4	5	6	7	8	9	10	11

127

G. Fill in the blanks with the appropriate spelling word.

1. The break between periods is only an __ __ __ __ __ __ __ __ __ __ __, not a real

   recess.

2. Part of fathers is the __ __ __ __ __ __ __ __ __ with Hanhalas Hamesivta.

3. Some __ __ __ __ __ __ __ __ __ __ highways are not long enough to actually leave the

   state.

4. Yosef Hatzadik had an __ __ __ __ __ __ __ __ __ __ __ __ when speaking to the rest of the

   Shevatim.

5. If an __ __ __ __ __ __ __ __ __ __ __ __ __ is returned for a touchdown, kids call it a 'pick

   six'.

6. The unnecessary comments __ __ __ __ __ __ __ __ __ the lesson.

7. There is __ __ __ __ __ __ __ __ __ __ __ __ __ competition between North Korea and

   the United States.

8. It took a long time for Lakewood Hatzoloh to arrange a __ __ __ __ __ __ __ __ __

   division.

9. __ __ __ __ __ __ __ __ lines do not meet.

10. I will __ __ __ __ __ __ __ __ __ __ this word if I say it a different way.

11. __ __ __ __ __ __ __ __ __ plants live throughout the year and usually bloom for a short

    period.

12. Hot water will __ __ __ __ __ __ __ __ __ __ through the ground beans for a brewed coffee.

13. Most notebooks are __ __ __ __ __ __ __ __ __ __ __ so the sheet can be detached cleanly.

14. There is __ __ __ __ __ __ __ __ __ conflict between Eisav and the Jewish people.

15.__ __ __ __ __ __ __ __ __ __ __ is necessary for success; it means sticking through

with it.

16.The president will __ __ __ __ __ __ __ __ his position if he resigns.

17.Getting sick will lead to your __ __ __ __ __ __ __ from school.

18.Yaakov Avinu was shown a glimpse of the __ __ __ __ __ __ __ __ __ __ __ at the

Mareh Hasulam.

19.Yaakov Avinu __ __ __ __ __ __ __ __ himself of sleep while learning in Yeshivas Shaim

V'Eiver.

20.The gas tank is __ __ __ __ __ __ __ __ when it shows 'empty'.

Key Concepts
- assimilated prefixes
- irregular spelling

The words assimilated is similar to similar. Surprise! That's because when something becomes similar to its surroundings it becomes assimilated, just like Jews in exile become assimilated when they begin to conform to and become similar to their gentile neighbors. A prefix becomes **assimilated** when the last letter changes to match the first letter of the root. This often happens because it is easier to repeat the same letter than to switch sounds in middle of the word. The word assimilated itself contains an assimilated prefix. The prefix **ad** means "toward" and **similate** means "the same or similar." It is much easier to pronounce **assimilated** than it is to pronounce **adsimilated** (and the **d** might not be noticeable), so the **d** assimilates to **s**.

But when that happens, it also becomes easier to misspell the word because you might forget that the consonant is doubled. It can help to remember the **Mad Ad** is in disguise when it assimilates.

The prefix **ad** is assimilated more than any other prefix. It also causes more double consonant spelling problems than any other prefix.

When there are exceptions to regular spelling rules they are called **irregular spellings**. Just like prefixes become assimilated in order to make the pronunciation of the words easier, other irregular spellings happen when joining some prefixes or suffixes because it is easier to pronounce the word that way.

Lesson Spelling Rule: The prefix **ad** is assimilated more than any other prefix. Remember to double the consonants because the first one is really the assimilated prefix.

Mnemonic device: Remember that one of the double consonants is really the **Mad Ad** in disguise.

Prefixes used in this lesson, together with their meanings:
- de- means under or away from
- ad- means to, towards or opposite
- re- means back or again
- pro- means forward or in support of
- ex- means out
- in- means within
- com- means with, all together

1. DE + CELERATE	=	DECELERATE
2. AD + CELERATE	=	ACCELERATE
3. RE + LOCATE	=	RELOCATE
4. AD + LOCATE	=	ALLOCATE
5. PRO + GRESSION	=	PROGRESSION
6. AD + GRESSION	=	AGGRESSION
7. DE + RIVE	=	DERIVE
8. AD + RIVE	=	ARRIVE
9. RE + SUME	=	RESUME
10. AD + SUME	=	ASSUME
11. EX + CUSE	=	EXCUSE
12. AD + CUSE	=	ACCUSE
13. IN + TENTION	=	INTENTION
14. AD + TENTION	=	ATTENTION
15. PRO + NOUNCE	=	PRONOUNCE
16. AD + NOUNCE	=	ANNOUNCE
17. RE + SENT	=	RESENT
18. AD + SENT	=	ASSENT
19. COM + PREHEND	=	COMPREHEND
20. AD + PREHEND	=	APPREHEND

Pay attention to the spelling words.

1. Do the words in each pair have the same root? _____ Do they have the same prefix?

_____

2. Look at the first word in each pair. Does the spelling of the prefix change when it is

added to the root? _____

3. What prefix is added to the second root in each pair? _____

4. How is the prefix spelled when it is joined to a root that begins with a **c**? _____ with an **l**?

_____ with a **g**? _____ with an **r**? _____ with an **s**? _____ with a **t**? _____ with an **n**?

_____ with a **p**? _____

5. Is it easier to pronounce **adtract** or **attract**? _____ **Adfection** or **affection**?

_____

The prefix **ad** is assimilated more than any other prefix. Remember to double the consonants because the first one is really the assimilated prefix.

131

Spelling Dictionary

1. **ac·cel·er·ate**   *v.* **–at·ed, –at·ing** to increase the speed of

2. **ac·cuse**   *v.* **–cused, –cus·ing** 1. to find at fault; to blame   2. to bring a lawsuit or charge towards (or against) someone

3. **al·lo·cate**   *v.* **–cat·ed, –cat·ing** to set apart for a specific purpose [to *allocate* funds for housing]

4. **ag·gres·sion**   *n.* 1. an unprovoked attack or warlike act   2. the practice or habit of being aggressive or quarrelsome   3. (Psychiatry) forceful or hostile behavior

5. **an·nounce**   *v.* **–nounced, –nounc·ing** to give notice of publicly; proclaim [to *announce* the opening of a new store]

6. **ap·pre·hend**   *v.* **–hend·ed, –hend·ing** 1. to capture or arrest [to *apprehend* a criminal]   2. to understand [to *apprehend* a problem]

7. **ap·pre·hen·sion**   *n.* 1. capture or arrest   2. a mental grasp or understanding   3. an anxious feeling or dread

8. **ap·pre·hen·sive**   *adj.* 1. able or quick to understand   2. uneasy or fearful about the future

9. **ar·rive**   *v.* **–rived, –riv·ing** to reach one's destination; come to a place   **–arrive at** 1. to reach by traveling   2. to reach by thinking [to *arrive* at a decision]

10. **as·sent**   *v.* **–sent·ed, –sent·ing** to say that one will accept an opinion, proposal, etc.; agree (to)

11. **as·sim·i·late**   *v.* 1. to become similar to one's environment   2. to make similar

12. **as·sume**   *v.* **–sumed, –sum·ing** 1. to take over; seize [to *assume* control]   2. to take for granted; suppose [we *assumed* that he was loyal]

13. **as·sump·tion**   *n.* 1. the act of assuming [an *assumption* of power]   2. anything taken for granted [our *assumption* of his innocence proved correct]

14. **at·tempt**   *n.* earnest and conscientious activity intended to do something   *–v.* **–tempted, –tempt·ing** 1. make an effort   2. enter into an activity

15. **at·ten·tion**   *n.* 1. the act of keeping one's mind closely on something   2. notice or observation [his smile caught my *attention*]   3. care or consideration

16. **cause**   *n.* 1. a justification for someting existing or happening   2. the event, force, or reason that generate something, or make it happen   3. a proceeding in a court of law whereby an individual seeks legal remedy   *–v.* **caused, caus·ing** to give rise to; make happen

17. **ce·ler·i·ty**   *n.* a rate that is rapid.

18. **com·pre·hend**   *v.* **–hend·ed, –hend·ing** to grasp mentally; understand

19. **com·pre·hen·sion**   *n.* the act of understanding or the power to understand

20. **com·pre·hen·sive**   *adj.* 1. including much; inclusive [a *comprehensive* survey]   2. able to comprehend fully [a *comprehensive* mind]

21. **con·sent**   *n.* 1. agreement   2. approval   *–v.* **–sent·ed, –sent·ing** 1. to agree (to do something)   2. to give permission or approval

22. **con·tend**   *v.* **–tend·ed, –tend·ing** 1. maintain or assert   2. argue about something; fight against

23. **de·cel·er·ate** *v.* to slow down

24. **de·rive**   *v.* **–rived, –riv·ing** to get or receive [we *derive* gasoline from petroleum; many people *derive* pleasure from music]

25. **dis·lo·cate**   *v.* **–cat·ed, –cat·ing** to put out of place; specif., to displace (a bone) from its proper position at a joint

26. **e·gress**   *n.* the act becoming visible, aparent   *–v.* **–gressed, –gress·ing** to come out of

27. **ex·cuse**   *v.* **–cused, –cus·ing** 1. to give reasons in defense of [she *excused* herself for being late]   2. to think of as not important; overlook; pardon [They *excused* his tardiness]   *–n.* a pretended reason; pretext

28. **grade**   *n.* 1. body of students who are taught together   2. a number or letter indicating quality (esp. of a student's performance)   3. a position on a scale of intensity or amount or quality   *–v.* **graded, grad·ing** assign a rank or rating to; determine the grade of

29. **in·sen·si·tive**   *adj.* not sensitive; having little or no reaction (to) [*insensitive* to music]

30. **in·ten·tion**   *n.* aim or purpose

31. **lo·ca·tion**   *n.* position; place; situation [a fine *location* for a Seforim store]

32. **lo·co·mo·tion**   *n.* motion, or the power of moving, from one place to another

33. **nun·cius**   *n.* 1. a messenger   2. the information communicated by a messenger; message

34. **pre·sume**   *v.* **–sumed, –sum·ing** 1. to take upon one's self without permission; venture [I wouldn't *presume* to tell you what to do]   2. to take for granted; suppose [I *presume* you know the risk you are taking]

35. **pro·gre·ssion**   *n.* 1. a moving forward or onward   2. a succession, as of acts, happenings, etc. [a *progression* of lucky events led to his success]

36. **pro·nounce**   *v.* **–nounced, –nounc·ing** 1. to say or declare officially, solemnly, etc.   2. to utter in the accepted or standard manner [he couldn't *pronounce* my name]

37. **pro·nounce·ment**   *n.* a formal statement of a fact, opinion, or judgment

38. **pro·nun·ci·a·tion**   *n.* 1. the act or manner of pronouncing words   2. the way a word or language is customarily spoken

39. **re·cuse**   *v.* **–cused, –cus·ing** to disqualify oneself (as a judge) from a particular case

40. **re·gress**   *v.* **–gressed, –gress·ing** to go back.

41. **re·lo·cate**   *v.* **–cat·ed, –cat·ing** to move to a new location

42. **rep·re·hend**   *v.* express strong disapproval of

43. **re·sent**   *v.* **–sent·ed, –sent·ing** to feel or show bitter hurt or anger at or toward [he *resented* being called a coward]

44. **re·sent·ment**   *n.* a feeling of bitter hurt or anger at being insulted, slighted, etc. [his great *resentment* at being left out]

45. **re·sume**   *v.* **–sumed, –sum·ing** 1. to take or occupy again [to *resume* one's seat] 2. to begin again or go on with after interruption [to *resume* a conversation]

46. **re·sump·tion**   *n.* the act of resuming [*resumption* of classes after vacation]

47. **ri·val**   *n.* the contestant you hope to defeat   *–v.* **–valed** or **–valled, –val·ing** or **–val·ling** 1. be equal to in quality or ability 2. be in competition with

48. **sen·sory**   *adj.* of the senses or sensation

49. **sen·ti·ment**   *n.* tender feeling or emotion

50. **sentimental**   *adj.* 1. having or showing tender or gentle feelings, often in a foolish way [a *sentimental* song] 2. of or resulting from sentiment [to save a picture for *sentimental* reasons]

51. **sum**   *n.* 1. the whole amount 2. the result gotten by adding numbers or quantities   *–v.* **–summed, –sum·ming** 1. to add up 2. to summarize

So how do the prefixes and roots all add up to the definitions?

DECELERATE   The root **celere** means "swift." Combined with **de**, which means "down, away, or undo," it means "to slow down" (the opposite of going swift).

ACCELERATE   **Ad** means "toward." So to **accelerate** is "to go toward with swiftness, or to speed up."

CELERITY is a word that shares the root **celere** and means "a rate that is rapid."

RELOCATE   The root **locare** means "place." **Re** means "back or again." So to **relocate** is "to move to another place."

ALLOCATE   The root **ad** means "toward." So to place something towards a purpose is to **allocate** it.

LOCATION is a word that shares the root **locare** and means "place."

PROGRESSION   **Gradere** means "to step, or to go." **Pro** means "forward." So to step forward is **progression**.

AGGRESSION   **Ad** can mean opposite. So to step opposite or against someone is **aggression**.

REGRESS is a word that shares the root **gradere** and means "to go back."

EGRESS is another word that shares the root **gradere** and means "exit."

GRADE, meaning level, ultimately comes from the root **gradere** and has the meaning "step".

DERIVE   The root **rive** comes from a stream or river and means "to lead or draw off." **De** means "away." So to lead away is to derive.

ARRIVE   The prefix **ad** means "toward" and to draw off toward the destination is to **arrive**. Another possibility is that it does not share the root with derive; but rather comes from the root **ripa**, meaning "shore." In that case, arriving means "going toward shore."

RIVAL, meaning opponent, ultimately comes from **rive**, and has the meaning "using the same stream as another."

RESUME   **Re** means "again" and **sumere** is "to take or add up," so to take up again is to arriving.

ASSUME   **Ad** is "toward" and **sumere** is "to take up," so to take toward an opinion before you know the evidence is to **assume**.

SUM is a word that shares the root **sumere** and means "total, or all of the parts."

PRESUME is another word that shares the root **sumere** and means to assume something before it is going to be proved.

EXCUSE   The root **causa** means "charge or lawsuit," and **ex** means "out." So to get out of being charged in a lawsuit is to **excuse**.

ACCUSE   Combining the root **causa** (lawsuit) with **ad** (against), leads to the word **accuse** meaning "to bring a lawsuit or charge towards (or against) someone."

RECUSE is a word that shares the root **causa** and joins to the prefix **re** (hold back) means to disqualify oneself from a lawsuit.

CAUSE is another word that shares the root **causa** and means a reason, or a lawsuit.

INTENTION   The root **tendere** means "to stretch," and (surprisingly!) **in** means "in"; so to stretch yourself in to doing something is **intention**.

ATTENTION   Joining the prefix **ad** (toward) to the root **tendere** (to stretch or exert) gives **attention** the meaning "to stretch yourself towards something."

CONTEND is a word that shares the root **tendere** and means to stretch together for something

ATTEMPT is another word that shares the root **tendere** [although the sounds **nd** changed to **mp**] and joined with the assimilated **ad** (toward) means "to try something."

PRONOUNCE   The root **nuntius** is "messenger," and **pro** means "forward." So when you send a message forth to the public, you **pronounce** it.

ANNOUNCE   Since the prefix **ad** (toward) is very similar to **pro** (forward) and it is joined to the root **nuntius**, the meaning is very similar to pronounce.

NUNCIUS is a word that nearly directly comes from the root **nuntius** and means "messenger or message."

RESENT   **Re** (again) joins with **sentir**, which means "to feel." So to feel pain and hurt again and again is to **resent**.

ASSENT   Ad (toward) joins with **sentir** (to feel) and gives the word **assent** the meaning "to feel towards something, to give approval towards a request."

SENTIMENT is a word that shares the root **sentir** and means feeling.

COMPREHEND   The root **prehend** is "to hold," and **com** is "together or intensely," so to hold intensely is to **comprehend**.

APPREHEND   Ad (toward) joined to **prehend** (hold) gives **apprehend** the meaning "to chase towards someone and then to catch hold of them."

REPREHEND is a word that shares the root **prehend**, and means "to strongly disapprove, to hold back."

The prefix **ad** means towards (or opposite) and often *assimilates* (ad + similar) to the letter that follows it when combined with a root. That means that the **d** changes to the first letter of the root to which it is joined.

Practicing the words
A. Complete each sentence with two spelling words that have the same root.

1. When you _____ announce the winners' names, _____ each

 name carefully.

2. A careful driver knows when to _____ and when to _____.

3. We _____ much pleasure from watching the ships _____ at port.

4. Do you _____ the fact that I gave my _____ to the idea?

5. The city will _____ funds to _____ the historic building.

6. You should _____ that classes will _____ on schedule.

7. No one could _____ why it is taking so long to _____ the

 criminal.

8. Attracting so much _____ was not my _____.

9. An unusual _____ of events finally led to an act of _____.

10. Did Robert _____ you of making up an _____?

B. Proofreading

Mrs. Mixit has done it again. She has mixed up the wrong prefix with the right root. Help her say what she really means by rewriting the nine underlined words correctly. Keep the root, but replace the prefix.

It has come to my <u>intention</u> that the birdbath at the corner of Maple and Second Streets is the victim of <u>progression</u>! Too many speeding cars <u>decelerate</u> as they pass the birdbath. The birds used to <u>arrive</u> great pleasure from this birdbath. But now they refuse to go near it, and we have a very dirty bird population! We can surely <u>resume</u> that they must <u>assent</u> all the noise and fumes from speeding cars. There is no <u>accuse</u> for this situation. The police have promised to <u>comprehend</u> any illegal speeders in the area. However, I suggest that the city <u>allocate</u> the birdbath to a nearby park. Remember, a happy, well-groomed bird is a fine, feathered friend!

_____	_____	_____
_____	_____	_____
_____	_____	_____

C. Read the meaning of the following roots. Then write the spelling words that contain these roots and match the definitions below. Checking the meaning of the prefix will help you decide if you have chosen the right word.

gress – to go   **celer** – swift   **sen** – feel   **loc** – place

1. to move to a different **place**

   _____

2. to go at a **swifter** speed

   _____

3. to **feel** agreement with

   _____

4. a **going** forward to attack

   _____

5. to **feel** hurt or anger

   _____

6. **place** or set apart for a purpose

   _____

7. slow down from a **swift** speed

   _____

8. a series **going** forward

   _____

D. Some words have a form that follows an irregular spelling pattern. This means that they are exceptions to the general spelling rules. The dictionary lists these words as separate entries. The following words are irregular when joined with some suffixes. Find the correct spelling and write them correctly on the line. Then answer the questions below.

1. resume + tion _____

2. assume + tion _____

3. comprehend + ive _____

4. comprehend + ion _____

5. apprehend + ive _____

6. apprehend + ion _____

7. pronounce + ment _____

8. pronounce + iation _____

9. In which four words does the d in the base form change to s? _____

_____ _____ _____

10. Which two word forms add the letter p? _____

_____

11. Which form drops an o from the base word? _____

12. In which word is the spelling regular? _____

140

E. Build a word pyramid by following the code. Use the spelling dictionary to find the four pyramid words that match the definitions.

The root **loc** means "place" or "put."

1. to put out of place

_____

2. to put aside for a specific purpose

_____

3. the power of moving from place to place

_____

4. to move to a new place

_____

		L	O	C								
		L	O	C	1	5	3					
	8	5	L	O	C	8	11	3				
		L	O	C	8	11	4	8	7			
	9	3	L	O	C	8	11	3	2			
2	4	10	L	O	C	8	11	3				
		L	O	C	8	6	8	11	4	8	7	

A	D	E	I	L	M	N	O	R	S	T
1	2	3	4	5	6	7	8	9	10	11

F. Build another word pyramid. Find the four pyramid words that match the definitions.

The root **sen** means "feel."

1. a feeling of hurt or anger

_____

2. of the senses or feelings

_____

3. having or showing tender feelings

_____

4. showing no feelings

_____

		S	E	N								
	1	11	S	E	N	12						
		S	E	N	11	9	10	14				
2	9	8	S	E	N	12	4	3				
	10	4	S	E	N	12	7	4	8	12		
		S	E	N	12	5	7	4	8	12	1	6
5	8	S	E	N	11	5	12	5	13	4		

A	C	D	E	I	L	M	N	O	R	S	T	V	Y
1	2	3	4	5	6	7	8	9	10	11	12	13	14

141

G. Fill in the blanks with the appropriate spelling word.

1. Give yourself enough space to __ __ __ __ __ __ __ __ __ in time to avoid an

   accident.

2. Press on the gas to __ __ __ __ __ __ __ __ __ __ quickly.

3. When משיח comes, בתי מדרש and בתי כנסת will __ __ __ __ __ __ __ __ to

   Yerushalayim.

4. We __ __ __ __ __ __ __ __ מעשר money to give to צדקה.

5. The __ __ __ __ __ __ __ __ __ __ __ of anti-Semitic hate is frightening.

6. Yiddin rarely should show __ __ __ __ __ __ __ __ __ __ when dealing with gentiles.

7. If you understand the meanings of prefixes, you can easily __ __ __ __ __ __ the

   meaning of many words.

8. If you have a good GPS, you should __ __ __ __ __ __ in time.

9. After Chanukah, we __ __ __ __ __ __ our schedule of studies.

10. I __ __ __ __ __ __ that you prefer better grades.

11. There is no __ __ __ __ __ __ to misspell the words rewritten in the second column.

12. Do not __ __ __ __ __ __ anyone falsely.

13. I am sure you have __ __ __ __ __ __ __ __ __ to achieve your utmost.

14. If you pay __ __ __ __ __ __ __ __ __, you will learn more.

15. A baal koyreh must do his best to __ __ __ __ __ __ __ __ __ the words correctly.

16. During Shacharis, the gabbai does not __ __ __ __ __ __ __ __ 'על הניסים' because it is a

    הפסק.

17. If you __ __ __ __ __ __ something, you risk transgressing לא תטור.

18. She indicated her __ __ __ __ __ __ with a nod of her head.

19. When you understand prefixes, it becomes easy to __ __ __ __ __ __ __ __ __ __ the language.

20. The police will not rest until they __ __ __ __ __ __ __ __ __ the criminal.

Spelling Lesson 14

Key Concepts
- hard and soft letters
- singular and plural nouns
- noun verb agreement
- plural forms of verbs
- present tense
- possessive form of nouns

A **hard** letter sound is one that is short and explosive, that comes out of the mouth with a popping sound. It cannot be lengthened for an appreciable amount of time. Some examples of hard sounds are **b**, **d**, and **k**.

A **soft** sound is one that comes out of the mouth along with air in a sort of hissing sound. It can be short or lengthened without changing its sound. Some examples of soft sounds are **ch**, **s**, and **th**.

A number of letters have both hard and soft sounds, like **c**, **g**, and **t**. Whether a letter sound is soft or hard usually depends on the following letter. If the letter is followed by a consonant, **a**, **o**, or **u** it will usually be a hard sound, but if it is followed by an **e**, **i**, or **y** it will usually be a soft sound.[26]

A **singular** noun is one that refers to an individual or an entire group as if it were an individual. When you use a singular noun the rest of your sentence must also be in singular tense. This is called **noun verb agreement**. The verbs must be in single tense to be in harmony and "agree" with the singular noun.

Most singular nouns change to **plural** by simply adding **s** to the end of the singular form. Sometimes you need to add **es**, sometimes change the end of the singular form slightly, and sometimes there are irregular plural forms. Whenever you are using a plural noun you must make sure that you also use the plural tense of the verbs to be in agreement.

The rules for single and plural for verbs when talking about doing something in the present tense is just about the opposite of nouns. **Present tense** means doing something right now, as opposed to past tense which means that it was already done or future tense which means that it will be done later. The plain form of the verb is usually good for plural in the present tense (for example, they **give** and **take**) but **s** needs to be added to form the singular present tense (he **gives** and **takes**).

To show that something belongs to a noun you need to use the **possessive** form of the noun. Add **'s** to all singular nouns and to a plural noun that does not end in **s** to form the possessive form (girl+**'s** = girl's, men+**'s** = men's). To a plural noun that ends in **s**, just add an apostrophe after the **s** (writers+**'** = writers').

Lesson Spelling Rule: When the letters **c** and **g** have a soft sound, they are usually followed by an **e**, **i**, or a **y**.
When the letters **c** and **g** have a hard sound, they are usually followed by an **a**, **o**, **u**, or any consonant except **y**.

Mnemonic device: Many word end with the letters **cle** (recycle, miracle, vehicle) or **gle** (angle, jungle, untangle). Remember that these endings cannot be spelled **cel** or **gel** without changing the sound of **c** and **g**.

---

26 There are always exceptions to every rule. The **g** in **get** and **give** is hard even though it is followed by **e** and **i**. The **c** in **facade** is soft even though it is followed by **a**.

1. CITIZEN
2. COURAGE
3. CONCERNED
4. URGENCY
5. LICENSE
6. MAGICIAN
7. CALENDAR
8. CATEGORY
9. CUSTOM
10. GUARANTEE
11. CEREAL
12. GUARD
13. CERTAIN
14. DIGESTION
15. CIRCUMSTANCE
16. FRAGILE
17. RECYCLE
18. GYMNASIUM
19. RELUCTANT
20. GARGLE

Pay attention to the spelling words.
In this spelling list, the letters **c** and **g** have both a hard sound (<u>c</u>ake, <u>g</u>avel) and a soft sound (fa<u>c</u>e, page).

1. Find nine words that contain a soft **c**. Write the letter that follows the soft **c** in each word.

    _____ _____ _____ _____ _____ _____ _____ _____ _____

2. Find eight words that contain a hard **c**. Write the letter that follows the hard **c** in each word.

    _____ _____ _____ _____ _____ _____ _____ _____

3. Find six soft **g** sounds in the list. Write the letter that comes after every **g** that has a soft sound.

    _____ _____ _____ _____ _____ _____

4. Find five hard **g** sounds. Write the letter that follows each hard **g**.

    _____ _____ _____ _____ _____

5. Do the letters **c** and **g** have a hard or a soft sound when they are followed by a consonant?

    _____

6. By the letters **e**, **i** or **y**? _____
7. By the letters **a**, **o**, or **u**? _____

When the letters **c** and **g** have a soft sound, they are usually followed by an **e**, **i**, or a **y**.
When the letters **c** and **g** have a hard sound, they are usually followed by an **a**, **o**, **u**, or any consonant except **y**.

Many word end with the letters **cle** (recycle, miracle, vehicle) or **gle** (angle, jungle, untangle). Remember that these endings cannot be spelled **cel** or **gel** without changing the sound of **c** and **g**.

145

1. **cal·en·dar** *n.* a table or chart that shows the days, weeks, and months of a year

2. **cat·e·go·ry** *n.* a class or division in a system of classification [biology is divided into two *categories*, zoology and botany]

3. **ce·re·al** *n.* food made from grain, esp. breakfast food, as oatmeal or cornflakes

4. **cer·tain** *adj.* 1. sure; positive [I'm *certain* she's here] 2. not named or described [a *certain* person was just here – guess who]

5. **cir·cum·stance** *n.* 1. a fact or event connected with or forming part of a situation [what were the *circumstances* that led to his arrest?] 2. (pl.[27]) conditions affecting a person, esp. financial conditions [in comfortable *circumstances*]

6. **ci·ti·zen** *n.* a member of a state or nation who owes allegiance to it and is entitled to full civil rights

7. **con·cern** *n.* 1. an anxious feeling; worry 2. something that causes anxiety *–v.* **–cerned, –cern·ing** 1. be relevant to [there were lots of questions *concerning* his speech] 2. be on the mind of [I'm *concerned* about young people vaping]

8. **con·cerned** *adj.* 1. involved or interested 2. uneasy or anxious *–v.* past tense of concern

9. **cour·age** *n.* a willingness to face and deal with danger, trouble, or pain; bravery **–the courage of one's convictions** the courage to do what one thinks is right

10. **cus·tom** *n.* a usual practice or habitual way of behaving; habit

11. **di·ges·tion** *n.* the act or process of changing (food) in the stomach and intestines into a form that can be used by the body

12. **frag·ile** *adj.* easily broken, damaged, or destroyed; delicate [*fragile* china]

13. **gar·gle** *n.* 1. a liquid used for gargling 2. a gargling sound *–v.* **–gled, –gl·ing** to rinse (the throat) with a liquid kept in motion by slowly forcing out air from the lungs

14. **guar·an·tee** *n.* a pledge that something will be replaced if it is not as represented [thirty-day *guarantee* on the vehicle]

15. **guard** *n.* 1. the act or duty of watching over, protecting, and defending 2. a person or group that guards *–v.* **guarded, guard·ing** 1. to watch over and protect [shepherds guard their flocks by night] 2. to keep from escape or trouble

16. **gym·na·si·um** *n.* a room or building equipped for physical training and athletic sports

17. **li·cense** *n.* formal or legal permission to do something [a *license* to marry] *–v.* **cense cense** to give a license to or for; permit formally

18. **ma·gi·cian** *n.* an expert in magic

19. **re·cy·cle** *v.* **–cled, –cl·ing** to use again and again, as a single supply of water

20. **re·luc·tant** *adj.* not wanting (*to* do something); unwilling

21. **ur·gen·cy** *n.* an urgent quality or state; need for quick action

---

27 Pl. stands for plural. This indicates that this usage of the word is only in the plural form of the word.

Practicing the words
A. Find the missing vowels in each word. Then rewrite the word.

1. c __ t __ g __ r __   _____

2. c __ r __ __ l   _____

3. fr __ g __ l __   _____

4. c __ t __ z __ n   _____

5. g __ __ rd   _____

6. c __ st __ m   _____

7. g __ rgl __   _____

8. l __ c __ ns __   _____

9. __ rg __ nc __   _____

10. c __ rt __ __ n   _____

11. g __ mn __ s __ __ m   _____

12. c __ rc __ mst __ nc __   _____

13. c __ l __ nd __ r   _____

14. r __ l __ ct __ nt   _____

15. g __ __ r __ nt __ __   _____

16. m __ g __ c __ __ n   _____

17. c __ __ r __ g __   _____

18. r __ c __ cl __   _____

19. c __ nc __ rn __ d   _____

20. d __ g __ st __ __ n   _____

B. Plural forms of nouns

The singular form of a noun is usually changed to plural by simply adding **s**.

When the singular form of the noun ends in a sound that is similar to s, you must add es to the word. Examples of such sounds are **ch** (bench+**es** = benches), **s** (iris+**es** = irises), **sh** (brush+**es** = brushes), **x** (fox+**es** = foxes), and **z** (blintz+**es** = blintzes).[28]

Some words that end in o also need to add es (potato + **es** = potatoes).[29]

However, when the last letter is **y**, sometimes a slight change needs to be made to the base word. If the letter right before the **y** is a vowel, no change is needed and simply add the **s**. If the letter preceding the **y** is a consonant, then the **y** must be changed to an **i** and **es** must be added.

Some words that end with **f** or **fe** form the plural by changing **f** to **v** and adding **es**[30].

Write the plural form of the following words:

1. six	_____	17. couch	_____
2. kiss	_____	18. axe	_____
3. wish	_____	19. flash	_____
4. city	_____	20. valley	_____
5. knife	_____	21. day	_____
6. loss	_____	22. miss	_____
7. fox	_____	23. watch	_____
8. coach	_____	24. country	_____
9. flash	_____	25. toy	_____
10. life	_____	26. glass	_____
11. switch	_____	27. witch	_____
12. wife	_____	28. choice	_____
13. company	_____	29. spice	_____
14. box	_____	30. chimney	_____
15. scarf	_____	31. splash	_____
16. loaf	_____	32. half	_____

---

28 If the word already ends in **e**, just add **s** (axe+**s** = axes).

29· Unfortunately, there is no general rule for this, each word can be checked in a dictionary for the correct form.

30 Although this is not a hard and fast rule, generally, this needs to be done when the letter before the **f** is a consonant or it ends in **fe**.

33. ditch   _____

34. perch   _____

35. horse   _____

36. cry   _____

37. party   _____

38. place   _____

39. donkey   _____

C. Possessives

The possessive form of a noun shows that something belongs to it.

Add **'s** to all singular nouns and to a plural noun that does not end in **s** to form the possessive form (boy+**'s** = boy's, women+**'s** = women's). Even if the singular noun ends in **s** or **s** sound, still add **'s**. So Pinchos+**'s** = Pinchos's and Max+**'s** = Max's.

To a plural noun that ends in **s**, just add an apostrophe after the **s** (writers+**'** = writers').

Rewrite each phrase to show the possessive form of the underlined word.

1. The tricks of the <u>magician</u> _____

2. the ingredients of the <u>cereal</u> _____

3. the guarantee of the <u>saleswoman</u> _____

4. the gymnasium of the <u>home team</u> _____

5. the rights of the <u>citizens</u> _____

6. the calendar of the <u>secretary</u> _____

7. the uniform of the <u>guards</u> _____

8. the beginning of the <u>custom</u> _____

9. the category of the <u>children</u> _____

10. the license of the <u>driver</u> _____

Hard and soft letters.

Languages are often similar to each other, and even though Lashon Hakodesh is from Hashem, whereas other languages were made up by humans at the time of the Dor Haflagah, there are similarities between them. Lashon Hakodesh also has soft and hard letters. The letter ק is a hard letter, and the letter ס is a soft letter. There are also some letters that are sometimes hard and sometimes soft. For example, the ב in בראשית is a hard sound. The letter ב in the word ובהו is a soft sound. The way to know whether the sound s hard or soft is to pay attention to the דגש, the little dot inside the letter. If there is no דגש, the sound is soft; with a dot, it is hard. This type of דגש is called a דגש קל.

D. Alliteration

Alliteration is the repetition of beginning consonant sounds: **P**eter **P**iper **p**icked a **p**eck of **p**ickled **p**eppers. If the same consonant is used, but its sound changes (for example from hard to soft), that is not alliteration. For example, "curved ceilings" is not an example of alliteration because one of the words is a hard **c** and the other is soft.

Write alliterative sentences like the one below, that use the sounds of the letters **c** and **g**. Use as many spelling words as possible in a single sentence. The sentence can be just as nonsensical as the example below. Thinking of the sounds, and writing the sentences will help you to remember the correct spelling. Feel free to use the spelling words more than once, and not the entire sentence needs to be the alliterative sound. Try to come up with at least two sentences for **c** and **g**, each.

Concerned **c**onsumers **c**ontinually **c**omplained, **c**laiming **c**alendar **c**ustoms **c**aused **c**onsiderable **c**onfusion.

_____

_____

_____

_____

_____

_____

_____

_____

E. Fill in the blanks with the appropriate spelling word.

1. Not every __ __ __ __ __ __ __ has the right to vote.

2. It takes lots of __ __ __ __ __ __ __ to change a habit.

3. Agudas Yisroel is __ __ __ __ __ __ __ __ __ about government interference with religion.

4. The __ __ __ __ __ __ __ of the situation called for immediate attention.

5. A fishing __ __ __ __ __ __ __ is not required in NJ for someone under 16.

6. My old chavrusa sometimes performs as a __ __ __ __ __ __ __ __ – Amazing Aaron.

7. Some people get a new __ __ __ __ __ __ __ __ for the new solar year.

8. One __ __ __ __ __ __ __ __ of כתבי הקודש is נביאים.

9. Some have a __ __ __ __ __ __ to observe ניטל נאכט in January (6-7).

10. Selling a field with אחריות means giving a __ __ __ __ __ __ __ __ __ against prior שעבודים.

11. Some kinds of __ __ __ __ __ __ never have concerns of Chodosh.

12. __ __ __ __ __ __ Your Tongue is a book about Shemiras Halashon.

13. We are __ __ __ __ __ __ __ about the truth of Torah.

14. After the time of __ __ __ __ __ __ __ __ __ __, one can no longer recite a ברכה אחרונה.

15. A favorable __ __ __ __ __ __ __ __ __ __ __ __ caused his rescue.

16. Menorah oil cups are __ __ __ __ __ __ __ if they are made from glass.

17. Lakewood township requires people to __ __ __ __ __ __ __ certain materials.

18. The __ __ __ __ __ __ __ __ __ is where many free periods are spent.

19. Many students are __ __ __ __ __ __ __ __ __ to spend time working on homework.

20. To fight cavities, __ __ __ __ __ __ with antiseptic mouthwash.

Spelling Lesson 15

Key Concepts
- syllable
- dividing words
- hyphen
- accented syllable
- related words
- schwa

A **syllable** is a word part that has a single vowel sound. It might have more than one vowel (c<u>oa</u>t, h<u>o</u>pe) or it might have no vowel at all (fum<u>bl</u>ing). An easy way to help you distinguish the syllables of a word is to pay close attention to your mouth and chin as you clearly enunciate the word. Each separate movement of your jaw is a distinct syllable.

Sometimes a word needs to be **divided** at the end of a line of writing because there is insufficient space to fit the entire word. The word can be divided according to its syllables, separating between complete mouth movements so the reader can easily understand what you wrote. If a word has more than two syllables, it can be divided between any two of them. As you complete the first part of the word, write a **hyphen** (-) to show that the word is not finished, then complete the rest of the word on the next line. For example, in the word psychology, from lesson 7, there are three places the word can be divided. In most dictionaries, the words are actually divided according to their syllables. This shows you how to pronounce it properly, and also how you can divide it at the end of a line. This is how it looks psycholo-gy. There is no space between the first part of the word and the hyphen.

In most words with more than a single syllable, one of the syllables is pronounced with more stress than other syllables. For example, in the word example, the main stress is on the am, (like eggs AM pull). It would seem silly for someone to stress the first syllable (EGGS am pull) or the last syllable (eggs am PULL). The stressed syllable is called an **accented syllable**.

Words that share the same base word, but have different suffixes are called **related words**. Often, the pronunciation is similar, but sometimes the accented syllable shifts to a different location in some of the words and a different syllable becomes accented. With these words you can remember how to spell the word correctly by thinking of a different related word and how it is pronounced.

A vowel sound that is barely pronounced is called a **schwa**. Surprisingly enough, it is very similar to an actual שׁוא, from which it is derived. It only occurs in an unstressed syllable of a word and sounds like the e sound in the word the moment. It can be represented by any vowel, or even no vowel at all. In English the schwa sound can be a syllable by itself.[31] Examples of schwa are: **a**way, el**e**phant, cous**i**n, choc**o**late, s**u**pport, vin**y**l, rhy**th**m. When you have a word that has the schwa sound, it can be difficult to distinguish which vowel it represents.

In some base words, the final syllable is not accented and sounds like a schwa. You might not remember how to spell the word. Recalling related words, when the suffix causes that syllable to become accented, will remind you how to spell that sound.

Lesson Spelling Rule: Unstressed vowels can be difficult to identify, especially before the letter r. First, think of related forms in which the mystery vowel may be stressed. Then use other clues to help you distinguish **ar/or** and **ary/ory**:
The ending **ar** often follows the letter **l**.
The ordin<u>ary</u> **ary** is more common than **ory** and **ery**.
The ending **or** often refers to a person or occupation. Both **or** and **ory** frequently follow the letter **t**.

---

31   This is different from Lashon Hakodesh, where no שׁוא is its own syllable. A שׁוא נח נח is part of the syllable that begins with the נקודה before it (a תנועה) and a שׁוא נע begins the next syllable together with the following (יתד) נקודה.

1.	POPULAR	POPULARITY
2.	REGULAR	REGULARITY
3.	SOLAR	SOLARIUM
4.	FAMILIAR	FAMILIARITY
5.	SIMILAR	SIMILARITY
6.	EDITOR	EDITORIAL
7.	AUTHOR	AUTHORITY
8.	SUPERIOR	SUPERIORITY
9.	MAJOR	MAJORITY
10.	MINOR	MINORITY
11.	ORDINARY	ORDINARILY
12.	LIBRARY	LIBRARIAN
13.	TEMPORARY	TEMPORARILY
14.	SECRETARY	SECRETARIAL
15.	VOLUNTARY	VOLUNTARILY
16.	IMAGINARY	IMAGINATION
17.	NECESSARY	NECESSARILY
18.	HISTORY	HISTORICAL
19.	VICTORY	VICTORIOUS
20.	MEMORY	MEMORIAL

Pay attention to the spelling words.

1. Before the suffixes are added, what are the last two letters of the first five base words? _____

2. What are the last two letters of the base words 6-10? _____

3. Can you clearly distinguish the vowel before the final **r** in these two groups of words? _____

4. Think of how both forms of each word is pronounced. Are the vowels easier to identify before or after the suffixes are added? _____

5. What three letters come at the end of the base words 11-17? _____

6. What unstressed vowel becomes stressed when suffixes are added to these words? _____

7. Think of the way the last three words are pronounced. How many syllables does each word have? _____

8. If the unstressed vowel were not pronounced, how many syllables would these words *seem* to have? _____

Unstressed vowels can be difficult to identify, especially before the letter r. First, think of related forms in which the mystery vowel may be stressed. Then use other clues to help you distinguish **ar/or** and **ary/ory**:

> The ending **ar** often follows the letter **l**.
> The ordinary **ary** is more common than **ory** and **ery**.
> The ending **or** often refers to a person or occupation.
> Both **or** and **ory** frequently follow the letter **t**.

Spelling Dictionary

1. **al·le·gor·i·cal**   *adj.* 1. of or characteristic of allegory   2. that is or contains allegory
2. **al·le·go·ry**   *n.* a story in which people, things, and events have a hidden or symbolic meaning
3. **au·thor**   *n.* the writer (*of* a book, article, etc.)
4. **au·thor·i·ty**   *n.* 1. the power or right to give commands or make final decisions; jurisdiction   2. an expert whose opinion is considered reliable [an *authority* on music]
5. **def·i·nite**   *adj.* 1. exact and clear in meaning   2. certain; positive
6. **de·fin·i·tive**   *adj.* 1. that decides or settles in a final way; conclusive [a *definitive* answer]   2. most nearly complete and accurate [a *definitive* biography]
7. **dic·ta·tor**   *n.* a ruler with absolute power and authority, esp. a tyrant or despot
8. **dic·ta·tor·i·al** *adj.* of, like, or characteristic of a dictator; autocratic; tyrannical; domineering
9. **ed·i·tor**   *n.* 1. a person who prepares copy for publication by selecting, arranging, revising, etc.   2. the head of a department of a newspaper magazine, etc.
10. **ed·i·tor·i·al**   *adj.* of, by, or characteristic of an editor or editors   -*n.* a statement of opinon in a newspaper, etc. or on radio, etc.
11. **fa·mil·iar**   *adj.* 1. knowing about; closely acquainted (*with*) [he is *familiar* with the subject]   2. well-known; common [a *familiar* sight]
12. **fa·mil·i·ar·i·ty**   *n.* 1. intimacy   2. the fact of being closely acquainted (*with* something) [his *familiarity* with the subject makes him an expert]
13. **his·tor·i·cal**   *adj.* 1. of or concerned with history   2. that really existed or happened [*historical* persons and events]
14. **his·to·ry**   *n.* an acount of what has happened in the life of a people, country, institution, etc.
15. **i·mag·i·na·ry**   *adj.* existing only in the imagination; unreal
16. **i·mag·i·na·tion**   *n.* the act or power of creating mental images of what is not actually present or of what has never been
17. **in·fi·nite**   *adj.* lacking limits or bounds; extending beyond measure or comprehension; without beginning or end [the universe is not *infinite*]
18. **in·fi·ni·ty**   *n.* endless or unlimited space, time, distance, amount, etc.
19. **li·brar·i·an**   *n.* a person in charge of a library
20. **li·brar·y**   *n.* a room or building where a collection of books, periodicals, etc. is kept for reading or reference
21. **ma·jor**   *adj.* greater in size, amount, or extent [a *major* effort]; greater in importance or rank [a *major* poet]
22. **ma·jor·i·ty**   *n.* the greater part or larger number; more than half [the *majority* voted to adjourn]
23. **me·mo·ri·al**   *n.* anything meant to help people remember some person or event, as a statue, holiday, etc.
24. **mem·o·ry**   *n.* 1. the power, act, or process of bringing to mind facts or experiences 2. a person, thing, etc. remembered [the music brought back *memories*]

SYN. –memory refers to the ability or power of keeping in or bringing to mind past thoughts, images, ideas, etc. [to have a good *memory*]; **remembrance** applies to the act or process of having such events or things come to mind again [the *remembrance* of things in the past]; **recollection** implies a careful effort to remember the details of some event [his *recollection* of the campaign is not too clear]; **reminiscence** implies the thoughtful or nostalgic recollection of long-past events, usually pleasant ones, or the telling of these [he entertained us with *reminiscences* of his childhood]

25. **mi·nor**   *adj.* 1. *a)* lesser in size, amount, or extent [a *minor* accident] *b)* lesser in importance or rank [a *minor* official]   2. under full legal age

26. **mi·nor·i·ty**   *n.* 1. the lesser part or smaller number; less than half [a *minority* voted for the law]   2. a racial, religious, or political group smaller than the larger, controlling group

27. **nec·es·sar·i·ly**   *adv.* as a necessary result [cloudy skies do not *necessarily* mean rain]

28. **nec·es·sar·y**   *adj.* that cannot be done without; essential; indispensable [the food *necessary* to life]

29. **or·a·to·ry**   *n.* skill in public speaking

30. **or·a·tor·i·cal**   *adj.* of or characteristic of a skilled public speaker

31. **or·di·nar·i·ly**   *adv.* usually; as a rule

32. **or·di·nar·y**   *adj.* 1. customary, usual [the *ordinary* price is $10]   2. unexceptional; common; average

33. **pe·cul·iar**   *adj.* 1. particular; special [a matter of *peculiar* interest]   2. queer; odd; strange [things look *peculiar* through these dark glasses]

34. **pe·cu·li·ar·ity**   *n.* 1. a being peculiar   2. something that is peculiar, as a habit

35. **pop·u·lar**   *adj.* 1. common; widespread [a *popular* notion]   2. liked by very many people [a *popular* actor]

36. **pop·u·lar·i·ty**   *n.* the quality of being popular

37. **reg·u·lar**   *adj.* 1. usual; customary [he sat in his *regular* place]   2. consistent, habitual, steady, etc. [a *regular* customer]

38. **reg·u·lar·i·ty**   *n.* 1. the quality of being regular

39. **sec·re·tar·i·al**   *adj.* in the nature of a secretary

40. **sec·re·tar·y**   *n.* a person whose work is keeping records, taking care of correspondence, etc., as in a business office

41. **sen·a·tor**   *n.* a member of a senate

42. **sen·a·to·ri·al**   *adj.* of or relating to senators

43. **sim·i·lar**   *adj.* nearly but not exactly the same or alike

44. **sim·i·lar·i·ty**   *n.* a being nearly but not exactly the same or alike

45. **so·lar**   *adj.* 1. of or having to do with the sun   2. produced by or coming from the sun [*solar* energy]

46. **so·lar·i·um**   *n.* a glassed-in porch, room, etc. where people sun themselves

47. **su·pe·ri·or**   *adj.* 1. high or higher in order, rank, etc. [a *superior* officer]   2. above average in quality; excellent [a *superior* wine]

48. **su·pe·ri·or·i·ty**   *n.* the quality of being superior

49. **tem·po·rar·i·ly**   *adv.* in a temporary manner; not permanent

50. **tem·po·rar·y**   *adj.* lasting only for a time; not permanent

51. **vic·to·ri·ous**   *adj.* having won a victory; triumphant

52. **vic·to·ry**   *n.* 1. the decisive winning of a battle or war   2. success in any struggle [a football *victory*]

53. **vol·un·tar·i·ly**   *adv.* in a voluntary manner; of one's own free will or choice

54. **vol·un·tar·y**   *adj.* brought about by one's own free choice; given or done of one's own free will [*voluntary* gifts]

Practicing the words

A. Syllables

The following spelling words have been divided into separate syllables. Paying careful attention to the pronunciation of the words, find the accented syllable (the one that is stressed) and circle it. Then write the related spelling word and circle its accented syllable. Also indicate which part of speech it is by writing the abbreviation.

1. POP · U · LAR

    _____

2. REG · U · LAR

    _____

3. SO · LAR

    _____

4. FA · MIL · IAR

    _____

5. SIM · I · LAR

    _____

6. ED · I · TOR

    _____

7. AU · THOR

    _____

8. SU · PE · RI · OR

    _____

9. MA · JOR

    _____

10. MI · NOR

    _____

11. OR · DI · NAR · Y

    _____

12. LI · BRAR · Y

    _____

13. TEM · PO · RAR · Y

    _____

14. SEC · RE · TAR · Y

    _____

15. VOL · UN · TAR · Y

    _____

16. I · MAG · I · NAR · Y

    _____

17. NEC · ES · SAR · Y

    _____

18. HIS · TO · RY

    _____

19. VIC · TO · RY

    _____

20. MEM · O · RY

    _____

B. The words in each group are related in some way. Find and write a spelling word that fits into each group.

1. everyday, usual, common _____

2. vital, essential, required _____

3. writer, novelist, columnist _____

4. president, vice-president, treasurer _____

5. supreme, primary, leading _____

6. fanciful, unreal, mythical _____

7. geography, spelling, science _____

8. inferior, good, average _____

9. conquest, win, triumph _____

10. approved, current, liked _____

11. atomic, electric, nuclear _____

12. unimportant, lesser, trivial _____

C. Proofreading

An important part of good writing is learning to avoid wordy phrases. Improve this paragraph by substituting a spelling word for each of the eight underlined phrases.

In order to do research for a book about reporters, author Ted Bennet was spending a week at *The Daily Sun*. First, Ted met the <u>person who makes assignments and checks the news stories</u>. Then he was introduced to a real reporter who let him work alongside her. Ted noticed that there was a <u>lot that was the same</u> between writing books and news reporting. The <u>biggest part</u> of both writers' time is spent collecting facts. This means going on interviews, making phone calls, and checking information at the <u>place with all the books and records</u>. Both jobs also require skill and <u>the ability to imagine and create things</u>. However, <u>most of the time</u> the reporter is working to meet a tight deadline and is writing to fit a very strict format. Ted was not <u>knowledgeable about or comfortable</u> with this sort of system, and was glad that his job as as reporter was only <u>for a short time</u>. When the week was over, Ted returned thankfully to his book, full of admiration for the reporters he had met.

1. _____

2. _____

3. _____

4. _____

5. _____

6. _____

7. _____

8. _____

E. Writing
Find the word in each phrase that is a synonym (similar in meaning) to a spelling word. Write the spelling word. Expand each phrase into a sentence in which the synonym you found is replaced with the spelling word.

1. an expert on earthquakes   _____

_____

2. usually arrives on time   _____

_____

3. most of the students   _____

_____

4. willingly helped   _____

_____

5. a definite likeness between them   _____

_____

6. the article in Tuesday's newspaper   _____

_____

7. efficient clerical staff in the office   _____

_____

F. Circle the first letter of each word in the nonsense sentences below to find eight base words. Then add the suffixes.

1. Put each crocodile under lights in Avrohom's room.

   _____   + ity   = _____

2. Did Illana crochet the airplane that Osher rode?

   _____   + ial   = _____

3. Sarah eats nearly all the orange radishes.

   _____   + ial   = _____

4. Aharon lets Leah entertain giants on Reuvein's yacht.

   _____   + ical   = _____

5. Osniel readily accepted the old red yo-yo.

   _____   + ical   = _____

6. Dazzling exports frequently include natural, impressive, tremendous eggs.

   _____   + ive   = _____

7. If Nechama feels irritable, nothing is too enjoyable.

   _____   + y   = _____

8. Perhaps ants rent little iceboxes and motorcycles, enjoy nature, travel, and raise yams.

   _____   + ian   = _____

G. Fill in the blanks with the appropriate spelling word.

1. The program's __ __ __ __ __ __ __ __ __ made it an instant success.

2. Keeping סדרים with __ __ __ __ __ __ __ __ __ __ is an essential habit for גשטיי\ing.

3. A יאהרציי\ candle is a type of __ __ __ __ __ __ __ __.

4. A __ __ __ __ __ __ __ __ might contain delicate plants or amphibians.

5. He addressed the דרשן with __ __ __ __ __ __ __ __ __ __ because they were related.

6. Making a דרשה from a __ __ __ __ __ __ __ __ __ __ is often called a בנין אב.

7. The __ __ __ __ __ __ __ __ __ __ duties are handled in a separate office.

8. He __ __ __ __ __ __ __ __ __ __ gave up his seat for the elderly gentleman.

9. I try to use my __ __ __ __ __ __ __ __ __ __ __ when composing these sentences.

10. They do not __ __ __ __ __ __ __ __ __ __ indicate ingenuity.

11. Using a number of pseudonyms, someone can write more than one __ __ __ __ __ __ __ __ __ in each issue of his newspaper.

12. His extensive research made him an __ __ __ __ __ __ __ __ __ on מקוואות.

13. The __ __ __ __ __ __ __ __ __ __ __ of the בד"ץ עדה החרדית makes it a very sought-after השגחה.

14. The __ __ __ __ __ __ __ __ __ of מחמירים will usually rely on the עדה החרדית.

15. There is a __ __ __ __ __ __ __ __ of people in חוץ לארץ who still איבער-מעשר.

16. __ __ __ __ __ __ __ __ __ __, we do not assume the produce was imported from ארץ ישראל.

17. The __ __ __ __ __ __ __ __ __ is responsible for keeping track of the books

18. The library is __ __ __ __ __ __ __ __ __ __ __ closed for mid-winter vacation.

19. There is __ __ __ __ __ __ __ __ __ __ debate about where קריעת ים סוף actually took place.

20. If you learn תורה with all your might you will be __ __ __ __ __ __ __ __ __ __ over your יצר הרע.

Key Concepts
- 1·1·1 words
- 1·1·1 doubling rule
- consonants and vowels
- VAC words or the 2·1·1 rule
- long vowels and short vowels
- idiom

The 1·1·1 doubling rule of spelling applies to **1·1·1 words**. These are short words that have a single syllable, a single vowel, and a single final consonant (for example **glad**). A syllable is a word part that has a single vowel sound and is made with a single movement of the chin and jaw. Once you determine that the word only has a single syllable, it must also have only one vowel. Words like **boat** or **hope** are not 1·1·1 words because they both contain more than one vowel. After determining that the word contains only one vowel, it must end in a single final consonant. **Help** and **lamp** are not 1·1·1 words because they end in two consonants.

A **vowel** is a sound that is made with the open throat or mouth and is like a נקודה. A **consonant** is any other letter sound.

The **1·1·1 doubling rule** means that when you add a suffix that begins with a vowel to a 1·1·1 word, you must double the final consonant of the base word (glad+er = gladder). This is an exception to the usual rule that when adding a suffix, no change is needed to the base word. If the suffix begins with a consonant, then there is no need to double the final letter of the base word (glad+**ly** = gladly).

If a word has more syllables, but the final syllable is accented and contains a single vowel with a single final consonant, the same rule applies. These are called VAC words: they end in a syllable that is **a**ccented, contains a single **v**owel, and a single final **c**onsonant. Another way to look at it is the 2·1·1 rule. The word has 2 (or more) syllables, the word ends in 1 consonant that is after 1 vowel and the ending is stressed (accented). For example, **commit** has more than a single syllable, but ends in 1 consonant after 1 vowel. So commit+**ing** = committed, but commit+**ment** = commitment.

A **long vowel** is a vowel sound that is made the same way as the vowel letter is called in the English language. For example, the letter **a** (sounds like eight) in the word **late** is a long vowel.

A **short vowel** is a vowel sound that is not made the same way as the vowel's letter name is. For example, the **a** in **apple** is a short vowel. Because each vowel has only one name, there is only one way to pronounce each long vowel. In contrast, there are numerous ways of pronouncing the short vowels because there are a lot of ways to be different from the long vowel. Some examples of different short **a**'s: amount, absolute; elephant; are.

The reason behind the 1·1·1 rule is because the silent e at the end of most words makes the vowel before it a long vowel. Since the usual rule for adding suffixes beginning with a vowel to a base word ending in silent e is to drop the e – remember way back in lesson 1 and 2 – it would become very confusing with 1·1·1 words (which do not have a silent final e) that also got a suffix beginning with a vowel. That is why the final consonant of the base is doubled, it clearly shows that the vowel was, and remains, a short vowel.[32]

Lesson Spelling Rule: Double the final consonant of a 1·1·1 word (or 2·1·1 word) before a suffix that begins with a vowel. Do not double before a suffix that begins with a consonant.

---

32 Because of this, if the 1·1·1 word contains a long vowel, it is an exception and you do not double the final consonant. For example, throw+ing = throwing.

Base Word	+ ED, ER	+ ING, EST, ARY, ANCE, ENCE, ENT, ABLE, AL	suffix beginning with consonant
1. FIT	FITTED	FITTING	FITNESS
2. THIN	THINNER	THINNEST	THINNESS[33]
3. MAD	MADDER	MADDEST	MADLY
4. THROB	THROBBED	THROBBING	
5. SUM	SUMMED	SUMMARY	
6. ZIP	ZIPPED, ZIPPER		
7. QUIT[34]	QUITTER	QUITTING	
8. ADMIT	ADMITTED	ADMITTANCE	
9. REMIT	REMITTED	REMITTANCE	
10. PERMIT	PERMITTED	PERMITTING	
11. OMIT	OMITTED	OMITTING	
12. SUBMIT	SUBMITTED	SUBMITTING	
13. OCCUR	OCCURRED	OCCURRENCE[35]	
14. RECUR	RECURRED	RECURRENCE	
15. CONCUR	CONCURRED	CONCURRENT	
16. REGRET	REGRETTED	REGRETTING	
17. ACQUIT	ACQUITTED	ACQUITTAL	
18. EQUIP	EQUIPPED	EQUIPPING	EQUIPMENT
19. ANNUL	ANNULLED	ANNULLING	ANNULMENT
20. COMMIT	COMMITTED	COMMITTING	COMMITMENT

> Double the final consonant of a 1·1·1 word (or 2·1·1 word) before a suffix that begins with a vowel. Do not double before a suffix that begins with a consonant.

Pay attention to the spelling words. The words on this list all fall under the 1·1·1 rule or the 2·1·1 rule.

1. Which words are 1·1·1 words? _____ Which are 2·1·1 words? _____
2. What happens to the final consonant of these words when a suffix beginning with a

   vowel is added? _____
3. What happens when a suffix beginning with a consonant is added?

   _____
4. In what three words are the letters **qu** treated as a single consonant?

   _____ _____ _____

---

33 Since the suffix also begins with an **n**, there ends up being two **n**'s, but it is not because of the 1·1·1 rule.
34 **Qu** is treated as a single consonant rather than a vowel. This is because the **u** tells you to add the **w** sound to the **k** of the **q**, and does not give instructions as to which way to pronounce that consonant sound of **kw**.
35 This is an exception to the general rule that **ance** is added to complete words and that **ence** is added to roots.

Spelling Dictionary

1. **ac·quit**   *v.* **–quit·ted, –quit·ting** to declare not guilty of a charge
2. **ac·quit·tal**   *n.* a setting free or being set free by a court
3. **ad·mit**   *v.* **–mit·ted, –mit·ting** 1. to permit to enter and use   2. to acknowledge or confess
4. **ad·mit·tance**   *n.* 1. an admitting or being admitted   2. permission or right to enter
5. **an·nul**   *v.* **–nulled, –nul·ling** 1. to do away with   2. to make no longer binding under the law [the marriage was *annulled*]
6. **an·nul·ment**   *n.* a formal statement by a court that a marriage is no longer binding
7. **com·mit**   *v.* **–mit·ted, –mit·ting** 1. to put officially in custody or confinement [committed to prison]   2. to do or perpetrate (an offense or crime)   **–commit to paper**[36] to write down
8. **com·mit·ment**   *n.* a pledge or promise
9. **con·cur**   *v.* **–curred, –cur·ring** 1. to combine in having an effect; act together   2. to agree (*with*); be in accord (*in* an opinion, etc.)
10. **con·cur·rent**   *adj.* 1. occurring or existing at the same time   2. in agreement
11. **e·quip**   *v.* **–quipped, –quip·ping** to provide what is needed; outfit
12. **e·quip·ment**   *n.* whatever one is equipped with for some purpose; supplies
13. **fit**   *v.* **fit·ted** also **fit·ed, fit·ting** also **fit·ing** 1. to be the proper size, shape, etc. for [the coat *fits* me]   2. to make or alter so as to fit [his new suit has to be *fitted*]   *–n.* the manner of fitting [a tight *fit*]   **–fit to be tied** (Colloq.) frustrated or angry
14. **fit·ness**   *n.* 1. good physical condition; being in shape or in condition   2. the quality of being suitable or qualified
15. **mad**   *adj.* 1. mentally ill; insane   2. foolish and rash; unwise [a *mad* scheme]   3. angry (often with *at*) [she's *mad* at us for leaving]
16. **mad·der**   *adj.* comparative[37] of mad
17. **mad·dest**   *adj.* superlative[38] of mad
18. **mad·ly**   *adv.* 1. insanely   2. foolishly   3. extremely
19. **oc·cur**   *v.* **–curred, –cur·ring** 1. to present itself; come to mind [an idea *occurred* to him]   2. to take place; happen [the accident *occurred* last week]
20. **oc·cur·rence**   *n.* something that occurs; event; incident
21. **o·mit**   *v.* **–mit·ted, –mit·ting** 1. to fail to include; leave out [to *omit* a name from the list]   2. to fail to do; neglect
22. **per·mit**   *v.* **–mit·ted, –mit·ting** to allow; consent to [smoking is not *permitted*]
23. **quit**   *v.* **quit** also **quit·ted, quit·ting** to stop, discontinue, or resign from [to *quit* one's job]   **–call it quits** to break off an attempt to do something; to end
24. **quit·ter**   *n.* a person who quits or gives up easily, without trying hard
25. **re·cur**   *v.* **–curred, –cur·ring** to happen or appear again or from time to time [his fever *recurs* every few months]
26. **re·cur·rence**   *n.* happening again (esp. at regular intervals) [the *recurrence* of spring]
27. **re·gret**   *v.* **–gret·ted, –gret·ting** to be sorry about or mourn for (a person or thing gone, lost, etc.)   *–n.* a troubled feeling or guilt   **–sent her regrets** a polite expression of regret as at refusing an invitation

---

36 When there is a common phrase that contains a word used differently from its literal meaning (called an idiom), the dictionary often lists the phrase under the entry of that word and defines the phrase.

37 Comparative is a form of comparison that means more than or having more of than.

38 Superlative is a form of comparison that means the best at or having the most of.

28. **re·mit** — *v.* **–mit·ted, –mit·ting** 1. to make less or weaker; slacken [without *remitting* one's efforts]   2. to send (money) in payment

29. **re·mit·tance** — *n.* money sent in payment, as by mail

30. **sub·mit** — *v.* **–mit·ted, –mit·ting** 1. to present to others for them to look over, decide about, etc.   2. yield

31. **sum** — *n.* 1. the whole amount   2.the result gotten by adding numbers or quantities   *–v.* **–summed, –sum·ming** 1. to add up   2. to summarize

32. **sum·mary** — *n.* a brief report covering the main points; digest

33. **thin** — *adj.* having little fat or flesh; slender

34. **thin·ner** — *adj.* Comparative of thin

35. **thin·ness** — *n.* the property of being thin

36. **thin·nest** — *adj.* Superlative of thin

37. **throb** — *v.* **throbbed, throb·ing** to beat strongly or fast; palpitate, as the heart under exertion   *–n.* a beat or pulsation

38. **zip** — *n.* (Colloq.) energy; force   *–v.* **zipped, zip·ping** (Colloq.) 1. to act or move with speed or energy   2. to fasten or unfasten with a zipper

39. **zip·per·** — *n.* a device used to fasten and unfasten two edges of material: it consists of two rows of interlocking teeth worked by a sliding part

Practicing the words
A. Form spelling words by adding endings to the base words.

1. Permit + ed   _____

2. fit + ness   _____

3. submit + ing   _____

4. mad + er   _____

5. annul + ment   _____

6. acquit + al   _____

7. submit + ing   _____

8. throb + ing   _____

9. regret + able   _____

10. mad + ly   _____

11. thin + nest   _____

12. zip + er   _____

13. annul + ment   _____

14. thin + ness   _____

15. quit + er   _____

16. recur + ed   _____

17. regret + ed   _____

18. concur + ent   _____

19. omit + ed   _____

20. sum + ary   _____

B. Answer each riddle with two spelling words that rhyme and belong in the spaces between the letters. Write the complete spelling words and the abbreviation of the part of speech.

1.   What did the criminal do when caught red-handed? ad__ed what he had com__ed

_____

2.   What did the coach give the baseball team? A com__nt to new equip__nt

_____

3.   What was the tired tailor always planning? qu__ng the f__ng

_____

4.   What would you call the second time an event happens? A re__ce of the o__ce

_____

5.   What do you call ticket money sent through the mail? The re__ce of the ad__ce

_____

6.   What was the teacher doing about overdue papers? per__ng late sub__ng

_____

7.   What did the confused judge do? co__ed the ac__ed

_____

8.   How was the astronaut prepared for his flight? He was eq__ed and z__ed

_____

9.   What did the witness say about the alleged crime? She c__ed that it o__ed

_____

C.

A **long vowel** is a sound that is the same as the vowel's name. For example, the letter **a** (sounds like eight) in the word **late** is a long vowel.

A **short vowel** is a sound that is not the same as the vowel's name. For example, the **a** in **apple** is a short vowel. Because each vowel has only one name, there is only one way to pronounce each long vowel. In contrast, there are numerous ways of pronouncing the short vowels because there are a lot of ways to be different from the long vowel. Some examples of different short **a**'s: amount, absolute; elephant; are.

Change the short vowel to a long vowel by adding a final silent **e** to each **1+1+1** word.

mad = _____   man = _____   sit = _____   dim = _____

mat = _____   plan = _____   shin = _____   rob = _____

When suffixes that begin with a vowel are added, **1+1+1** words and final silent **e** words are often confused. Write the correct **ing** form for each space.

1. grip/gripe   _____ the handlebars, he started _____ about the flat tire.

2. star/stare   Everyone was _____ at the actors who were _____ in the play.

3. scrap/scrape   Reuven considered _____ the old bicycle after _____ both fenders.

4. tap/tape   The loud _____ noise interrupted my _____ of the music.

5. wag/wage   He started _____ his finger when they spoke of _____ war.

6. mop/mope   If you don't stop _____ you'll never finish _____ the floor.

D. Idioms
An idiom is a phrase that has a meaning different from what the individual words usually mean. For instance, "flash in the pan" means "a sudden, seemingly skilled effort that fails." The meanings of idiomatic phrases are usually found in the entry for the key word of the idiom.

> **flash** *v.* to send out a sudden, brief light, esp. at intervals
> **–flash in the pan** 1. a sudden, seemingly skillful effort that fails   2. one that fails after such an effort

Each sentence contains an idiom. The key word in each idiom is a spelling word. First find the spelling word and look it up in the spelling dictionary. Then write the idiom and the definition for it that is shown in the entry.

1. Let's call it quits for today and finish the game tomorrow.

_____

_____

2. Your clever ideas should be committed to paper.

_____

_____

3. Shoshanah sent her regrets by mail.

_____

_____

4. Whenever it rains on a Sunday I am fit to be tied.

_____

_____

E. Fill in the blanks with the appropriate spelling word.

1. The crossing guard __ __ __ __ __ __ __ __ the emergency vehicle to go ahead.

2. The word __ __ __ __ __ __ __ __ with alarming frequency.

3. It is not __ __ __ __ __ __ __ for a בן תורה to walk about untucked.

4. The __ __ __ __ __ __ __ __ lines are written with the point of the קולמוס.

5. __ __ __ __ __ __ __ __ unnecessary words make for smooth reading in your writing.

6. Who is still __ __ __ __ __ __ __ __ __ __ their application to Mesivta?

7. Nearly every __ __ __ __ __ __ __ __ __ __ of the word 'very' is very unnecessary.

8. He chased after them __ __ __ __ __, in hot pursuit.

9. The opinion of the entire courtroom __ __ __ __ __ __ __ __ __ with the jury's verdict.

10. The loan becomes __ __ __ __ __ __ __ __ when שמיטה arrives – unless a פרוזבול was made.

11. It takes great __ __ __ __ __ __ __ __ __ __ to stick to the דף יומי schedule.

12. Their mistake was a __ __ __ __ __ __ __ __ __ __ __ incident.

13. His finger __ __ __ __ __ __ __ with the pain of infection.

14. The court martial dispensed __ __ __ __ __ __ __ justice.

15. The __ __ __ __ __ __ is a nifty invention.

16. __ __ __ __ __ __ __ __ is not an option.

17. __ __ __ __ __ __ __ __ __ __ of questionable evidence rendered the decision unjust.

18. He __ __ __ __ __ __ __ __ a list of his expenses for reimbursement.

19. The president's __ __ __ __ __ __ __ __ __ is nearly certain.

20. Among my __ __ __ __ __ __ __ __ __ are a number of sharp blades.

Key Concepts
- 2·1·1 rule
- accented syllable
- variant spelling

The **2·1·1 rule** of doubling final consonants applies to 2·1·1 words. 2·1·1 words have two or more syllables, end in a single consonant after a single vowel, and are accented on the final syllable. The 2·1·1 rule says that if you add a suffix beginning with a vowel to the 2·1·1 word, the final consonant is doubled.

An **accented syllable** is the part of the word that is stressed, or spoken with more emphasis. Another word for it is inflected syllable.

We already saw in lesson 15 that changing suffixes sometimes changes the inflection, or the accented syllable. The same thing can happen to 2·1·1 words. If adding a suffix moves the accent away from the final syllable in the base word, then the 2·1·1 rule does not apply.

Variant is another word for alternative. In language, variants are alternative forms of spelling, pronouncing, or saying a word. Some variants are just as common as each other, while others are less frequently used. The dictionary will often list the variant forms after the entry word that comes first alphabetically, or after the entry word that is used more commonly if it comes first. The way the dictionary tells you if they are just as common or one is more frequent is by using the words or and also. If it says or the variant, they are just as common. If it says also the variant, then the entry word is the more frequent one.

Sometimes variants are based on location where the language is spoken. For example Canada and Britain often differ from the United States. In this lesson, the words that end in l have variant spellings. In Canada and Britain the final l is often doubled.

Lesson Spelling Rule: The 2·1·1 rule only applies to a word that has its final syllable accented. If adding the suffix moves the accent away from that syllable, the 2·1·1 rule does not apply.

1. EXPEL	EXPELLED	EXPELLING	
2. REPEL	REPELLED	REPELLING	
3. PROPEL	PROPELLED	PROPELLING	
4. COMPEL	COMPELLED	COMPELLING	
5. DISPEL	DISPELLED	DISPELLING	
6. REFER	REFERRED	REFERRING	REFERENCE
7. INFER	INFERRED	INFERRING	INFERENCE
8. INFER	INFERRED	INFERRING	INFERENCE
9. CONFER	CONFERRED	CONFERRING	CONFERENCE
10. TRANSFER	TRANSFERED	TRANSFERING	CONFERENCE
11. PROFIT	PROFITED	PROFITING	
12. BENEFIT	BENEFITED	BENEFITING	
13. BENEFIT	BENEFITED	BENEFITING	
14. EDIT	EDITED	EDITING	
15. LIMIT	LIMITED	LIMITING	
16. MODEL	MODELED	MODELING	
17. LABEL	LABELED	LABELING	
18. TRAVEL	TRAVELED	TRAVELING	
19. CANCEL	CANCELED	CANCELING	
20. QUARREL	QUARRELED	QUARRELING	

Pay attention to the spelling words.

1. What syllable is accented in the first ten words? _____

2. What syllable is accented in the last ten words? _____

3. Which words are 2·1·1 words? _____

4. What happens to the final consonant of the 2·1·1 word when a suffix beginning with a vowel is

   added? _____

5. Some of the 2·1·1 words use the **ence** suffix. What syllable is accented in those words? _____

6. Why isn't the final consonant of the base word doubled? _____

7. Which word has more than one way to pronounce it? _____

8. In what way would its spelling change because of its pronunciation? _____

> The 2·1·1 rule only applies to a word that has its final syllable accented. If adding the suffix moves the accent away from that syllable, the 2·1·1 rule does not apply.

173

1.   **ben·e·fit**   *n.* anything helping to improve conditions [a paved road for the *benefit* of all the residents]   *–v.* to receive advantage; profit [he'll *benefit* from regular exercise]

2.   **can·cel**   *v.* **–eled** or **–elled, –el·ing** or **–el·ling** 1. to cross out with lines or mark over   2. to do away with; abolish, withdraw, etc. [to *cancel* an order]

3.   **chan·nel**   *n.* 1. a body of water joining two larger bodies of water   2. any means by which something moves or passes   3. the band of frequencies within which a radio or television transmitting station must keep its signal   *v.* **–eled** or **–elled, –el·ing** or **–el·ling** to send through a channel

4.   **com·pel**   *v.* **–elled, –el·ling** to force or oblige to do something

5.   **con·fer**   *v.* **–ferred, –fer·ring** 1. to give, grant, or bestow [to *confer* a medal upon the hero]   2. to meet for discussion

6.   **con·fer·ence**   *n.* a conferring or consulting on a serious matter

7.   **cred·it**   *n.* 1. praise or approval [to deserve *credit* for trying]   2. an official record that one has completed a unit or course of study   *–v.* to give credit to

8.   **dis·pel**   *v.* **–elled, –el·ling** to scatter and drive away [wind *dispelled* the fog]

9.   **ed·it**   *v.* 1. to prepare written material for publication by selecting, arranging, revising, etc.   2. to be in charge of what is printed in (a newspaper or periodical)

10.   **ed·i·tor**   *n.* 1. a person who prepares copy for publication by selecting, arranging, revising, etc.   2. the head of a department of a newspaper, magazine, etc.

11.   **e·mit**   *v.* **e·mit·ted, e·mit·ting** to send out; give forth [the kettle *emitted* steam]

12.   **ex·pel**   *v.* **–elled, –el·ling** 1. to drive out by force; eject [harmful gases *expelled* through the exhaust pipe]   2. to dismiss or send away by authority [he was *expelled* from school]

13.   **ex·tol**   *v.* **–elled, el·ling** to praise highly; laud

14.   **im·pel**   *v.* **–elled, –el·ling** 1. to push, drive, or move forward; propel   2. to force, compel, or urge [what *impels* him to lie?]

15.   **in·fer**   *v.* **–ferred, –fer·ring** to conclude by reasoning from something known or assumed

16.   **in·fer·ence**   *n.* a conclusion or opinion arrived at by inferring

17.   **la·bel**   *n.* 1. a card, strip of paper, etc. marked and attached to an object to show what it is   2, a descriptive word or phrase applied to a person, group, etc.   3. an identifying brand of a company   *–v.* **–eled** or **–elled, –el·ing** or   **–el·ling** 1. to attach a label to   2. to classify as; call; describe

18.   **lim·it**   *n.* 1. the point, line, or edge where something ends or must end [beyond the *limit* of his strength]   2. *pl.* bounds or boundaries [city *limits*]   *–v.* to set a limit to; restrict; curb

19.   **mar·vel**   *n.* a wonderful or astonishing thing   *v.* **–eled** or   **–elled, –el·ing** or **–el·ling** to be amazed; wonder

20.   **mod·el**   *n.* 1. a small copy of an object   2. a person or thing considered as a standard of excellence to be imitated   3. a style or design [a 1984 *model*]   4. a person who poses for an artist or photographer   *–adj.* 1. serving as a model, or standard of excellence [a *model* student]   2. representative of others of the same kind, style, etc.; typical [a *model* home]   *–v.* **–eled** or **–elled, –el·ing** or **–el·ling** 1. to make a model of   2. to display (a dress, etc.) by wearing

21.   **pan·el**   *n.* a flat piece forming part of the surface of a wall, door, etc.   *–v.* **–eled** or **–elled, –el·ing** or **–el·ling** to provide, decorate, etc. with panels

22.   **pre·fer**   *v.* **–ferred, –fer·ring** to choose first; like better [he *prefers* baseball to football

23. **preference**   *n.* a preferring; greater liking [a *preference* for lively music]

24. **pro·fit**   *n.* 1. advantage; benefit [it would be to his *profit* to read more] 2. *often pl.* income from money invested   *–v.* to make a profit; benefit; gain

25. **pro·pel**   *v.* **–lled, –el·ling** to push, drive, or make go onward, forward, or ahead [a rocket *propelled* by liquid fuel]

26. **quar·rel**   *n.* a dispute, esp. one marked by anger and resentment   *–v.* **–eled** or **–elled, –el·ing** or **–el·ling** to dispute heatedly

27. **rav·el**   *v.* **–eled** or **–elled, –el·ing** or **–el·ling** to separate the parts, esp. threads, of; untwist

28. **re·but**   *v.* **–but·ted, but·ting** to prove, or try to prove (someone or something) to be wrong

29. **re·fer**   *v.* **–ferred, –fer·ring** to direct (to someone or something) for aid, information, etc.

30. **ref·er·ence**   *n.* 1. a mention or allusion [she made no *reference* to the accident] 2. a statement giving the qualifications, abilities, etc. of someone seeking a position 3. a source of information [*reference* books]

31. **re·pel**   *v.* **–elled, –el·ling** 1. to drive back or force back [to *repel* an attack] 2. to cause dislike in; disgust [the odor *repels* me]

32. **trans·fer**   *v.* 1. to move, carry, send, etc. from one person or place to another 2. to change from one school, college, etc. to another 3. to change from one bus, train, etc. to another   *–n.* a ticket allowing the bearer to change from one bus, train, etc. to another

33. **trans·fer·ence**   *n.* 1. the act of transferring from one form to another 2. changing ownership

34. **trav·el**   *v.* **–eled** or **–elled, –el·ing** or **el·ling** 1. to go from one place to another; make a journey [they *traveled* across the state] 2. (*basketball*) to move (usually more than two steps) while holding the ball

35. **tun·nel**   *n.* 1. an underground or underwater passageway for automobiles, trains, etc. 2. an animal's burrow   *–v.* **–eled** or **–elled, –el·ing** or **–el·ling** to make a tunnel through

Practicing the words

A. Each base word in the first column is divided into syllables. Say each word to yourself and listen for the accented or inflected syllable – the one that you emphasize most. Circle the accented syllable. Then add the endings shown to the base word and write the word forms.

1. quar · rel   + ed = _____   + ing = _____

1. re · fer   + ed = _____   + ing = _____

2. prof · it   + ed = _____   + ing = _____

3. in · fer   + ed = _____   + ing = _____

4. tra · vel   + ed = _____   + er = _____

5. mod · el   + ed = _____   + ing = _____

6. con · fer   + ed = _____   + ing = _____

7. pro · pel   + ed = _____   + er = _____

8. ex · pel   + ed = _____   + ing = _____

9. ben · e · fit   + ed = _____   + ing = _____

10. pre · fer   + ed = _____   + ing = _____

11. re · pel   + ed = _____   + ent = _____

12. cred · it   + ed = _____   + ing = _____

13. can · cel   + ed = _____   + ing = _____

14. ed · it   + ed = _____   + or = _____

15. lim · it   + ed = _____   + ing = _____

B. Proofreading

Mrs. Mixit is still combining the wrong prefix with the right root. Help her say what she really means by writing the nine underlined words correctly.

I am honored to be the keynote speaker at this year's <u>inference</u> on gardening. First, I feel <u>repelled</u> to tell you that you should grow what you like and like what you grow. My personal <u>reference</u> is the petunia[39]. I feel myself <u>expelled</u> toward any garden where precious petunias are in bloom. However, I don't want you to make the <u>conference</u> that I like only petunias. My <u>preference</u> to petunias is just an example. I love most flowers and am not <u>propelled</u> by any single type. I'm sure you will have no trouble <u>conferring</u> the idea behind my example of petunias to your own taste in flowers. I hope I have <u>compelled</u> any incorrect notion. Now, where was I?

1. _____   4. _____   7. _____

2. _____   5. _____   8. _____

3. _____   6. _____   9. _____

---

39 A type of flower.

C. Read the definitions for **transfer**, **credit**, **editor**, **label**, and **travel** and use one word in each sentence below. You may add an ending to the word. Write the definition which best matches the word as you used it in the sentence.

1. When did that recording group switch to a new _____? _____

   _____

2. Who is the _____ of the morning newspaper? _____

   _____

3. You must take the final test to receive _____ for the course. _____

   _____

4. The bus driver asked to see our _____. _____

   _____

5. The referee called a penalty for _____ with the ball. _____

   _____

D. Using the letter maze, begin by writing the letter I on the first line. Then count every three letters to find nine new words that are similar to the ones in this lesson. Cross out each letter as you use it. You should go around the maze three times, and there will be one letter left over. Write the words on the lines.

M	➡	I	A	I	M	R	T	P	V	T	E	E
M												U
Z												L
E												L
L												N
L												E
T												P
E												N
E												X
U												A
N												E
V												T
B												N
N												L
	A	E	A	R	R	H	L	L	C	E	O	

1. ______________________________
2. ______________________________
3. ______________________________
4. ______________________________
5. ______________________________
6. ______________________________
7. ______________________________
8. ______________________________
9. ______________________________

Add **ed** or **ing** to the new words to match these definitions. Then answer the question.

1. showed wonder at ______________________________
2. praising highly ______________________________
3. forced to move forward ______________________________
4. directed into the proper place ______________________________
5. digging a passage through ______________________________
6. put up wall coverings ______________________________
7. giving off ______________________________
8. trying to prove something wrong ______________________________
9. untwisted, untangled ______________________________
10. Would you expect any of these forms to have a second spelling in the dictionary? Why?

____

E. Fill in the blanks with the appropriate spelling words.

1. He __ __ __ __ __ __ __ his breath with a sigh of relief.

2. Mosquito __ __ __ __ __ __ __ __ is really useful in the summer.

3. The fan's __ __ __ __ __ __ __ __ broke when it got knocked over.

4. The defense's __ __ __ __ __ __ __ __ __ argument won the trial.

5. The clear evidence __ __ __ __ __ __ __ __ all doubt.

6. The עין משפט makes __ __ __ __ __ __ __ __ to the רמב"ם, סמ"ג, and the שולחן ערוך about

    the גמ

7. The גמ' __ __ __ __ __ __ __ that ריב"ל held לשמה בקיאין שאין לפי.

8. Devorah's __ __ __ __ __ __ __ __ __ was to have fleishig for supper.

9. The hanhallah is __ __ __ __ __ __ __ __ __ a great distinction on the מסיים.

10. He __ __ __ __ __ __ __ __ __ from one bus line to the other.

11. Shifra was __ __ __ __ __ __ __ __ from her experiences as a waitress.

12. The rules __ __ __ __ __ __ __ __ the poor workers.

13. The company __ __ __ __ __ __ __ her account for the spoiled merchandise.

14. If you like catching mistakes, you might want to become an __ __ __ __ __ __.

15. Preserve your hearing by __ __ __ __ __ __ __ your exposure to loud music.

16. The teacher __ __ __ __ __ __ __ how to do the prewriting work on the board.

17. The sefer was clearly __ __ __ __ __ __ __ with the name of its owner.

18. I met the __ __ __ __ __ __ __ in the Bobov Bais Medrash near the bus stop.

19. Are you __ __ __ __ __ __ __ __ your subscription to the newsline?

20. Usually you should not be __ __ __ __ __ __ __ __ __ with classmates.

Key Concepts
- hard and soft letter sounds
- adjusting suffixes to keep the hard/soft sound
- pairs of suffixes

A hard sound is one that is short and explosive, that comes out of the mouth with a popping sound. It cannot be lengthened for an appreciable amount of time. Some examples of hard sounds are **b**, **p**, and **d**.
A soft sound is one that comes out of the mouth along with air in a sort of hissing sound. It can be short or lengthened without changing its sound. Some examples of soft sounds are **ch**, **s**, and **th**.

The letter or vowel that follows **c** or **g** usually indicate whether the **c** or **g** was hard or soft. Sometimes, the usual **rules for suffixes are adjusted in order to maintain the c or g as a hard or soft letter**. There are a few **pairs of suffixes** that each work the same way, but are spelled with a different vowel. That means that if the pair changes a verb to a noun, both suffixes will function the same way, but some words will get the version of the suffix with one vowel while others will get the one with the other vowel. These are: **ant/ent**, **able/ible**, **uous/ious**, **ance/ence**. When the suffix follows the letter **c** or **g**, make sure to use the version of the suffix that will keep the sound of the **c** or **g** soft or hard as the word is pronounced.

Lesson Spelling Rule: When the letters **c** or **g** have a hard sound, they will be followed by the vowels **a**, **o**, or **u**, or a consonant. When they are soft, they will be followed by the vowels **e**, **i**, and **y**.
The pairs of suffixes follow **c** or **g** the same way.
If the **c** or **g** is hard, use the endings ance ant, able, uous.
If the **c** or **g** is soft, use the endings ence, ent, ible, ious.
Sometimes the final silent **e** is kept to protect the soft sound of **c** or **g** when a suffix is added.

181

1. ELEGANT	5. INTELLIGENT	9. OUTRAGEOUS
2. EXTRAVAGANCE	6. NEGLIGENCE	10. VENGEANCE
3. NAVIGABLE	7. ELIGIBLE	
4. AMBIGUOUS	8. CONTAGIOUS	

11. APPLICANT	15. MAGNIFICENT	19. ENFORCEABLE
12. SIGNIFICANCE	16. INNOCENCE	20. REPLACEABLE
13. COMMUNICABLE	17. CONVINCIBLE	
14. CONSPICUOUS	18. SUSPICIOUS	

Pay attention to the spelling words.

1. Look at the words in the first column and think about their pronunciation. Do the underlined letters have a hard or a soft sound? _____

2. Write the endings that follow these letters _____ _____ _____ _____

3. Look at the words in the second column and think about their pronunciation. Do the underlined letters have a hard or a soft sound? _____

4. Write the endings that follow these letters _____ _____ _____ _____

5. When **c** or **g** has a hard sound, it is followed by which letters? ____ or ____

6. When **c** or **g** has a soft sound, it is followed by the letters ____ or ____.

7. When a final silent **e** is followed by a suffix beginning with a vowel, what usually happens to the **e**? _____

8. Look at the words in the final column. If the **e** were dropped in these words what vowel would follow the **c** and **g**? ____ Would its sound be soft or hard? _____

9. What is done with the final **e** to maintain the appropriate sound of **c** or **g** in this case? _____

10. It is often difficult to choose between the following endings when you are spelling a word: **ant/ent, ance/ence, able/ible, uous/ious**. When the letter before the ending is **c** or **g**, what can help you remember the appropriate ending?

_____

When the letters **c** or **g** have a hard sound, they will be followed by the vowels **a, o,** or **u,** or a consonant. When they are soft, they will be followed by the vowels **e, i,** and **y**.
The pairs of suffixes follow **c** or **g** the same way.
If the **c** or **g** is hard, use the endings ance ant, able, uous.
If the **c** or **g** is soft, use the endings ence, ent, ible, ious.
Sometimes the final silent **e** is kept to protect the soft sound of **c** or **g** when a suffix is added.

---

1. **am·big·u·ous**   *adj*. not clear; vague
2. **app·li·cant**   *n*. a person who applies, as for employment, help, etc.
3. **ap·ply**   *v*. –**plied, –ply·ing** 1. to put on [to apply salve]   2. to make a formal request [to *apply* for a job]   3. to be suitable or relevant [this rule *applies* to everyone]
4. **com·mu·ni·ca·ble**   *adj*. 1. that can be communicated, as an idea   2. that can be transmitted, as a disease
5. **com·mu·ni·cate**   *v*. –**cat·ed, –cat·ing** to give, exchange, speak
6. **com·mu·ni·ca·tion**   *n*. a giving or exchanging of information, etc. by talk, writing, etc.
7. **con·spic·u·ous**   *adj*. easy to see or perceive; obvious [a *conspicuous* poster]
8. **con·ta·gion**   *n*. 1. the spreading of a disease by contact   2. a contagious disease
9. **con·ta·gious**   *adj*. spread by contact: said of diseases
10. **con·vince**   *v*. –**vinced, –vinc·ing** to overcome the doubts of; persuade by argument [I'm *convinced* he's telling the truth]   —**con·vin·ci·ble** *adj*. —**con·vinc·ing·ly** *adv*.
11. **con·vin·ci·ble**   *adj*. subject to convincing
12. **el·e·gant**   *adj*. having a dignified richness and grace, as of dress, style, manner, etc. —**el·e·gant·ly** *adv*.
13. **el·i·gi·ble**   *adj*. fit to be chosen, qualified by law, rules, etc. [*eligible* to hold office] —**el·i·gi·bil·i·ty** *n*.   —**el·i·gi·bly** *adv*.
14. **en·force**   *v*. –**forced, –forc·ing** to force observance of (a law, etc.) —**en·force·a·ble** *adj*.   —**en·force·ment** *n*.
15. **en·force·a·ble**   *adj*. subject to being enforced
16. **ex·trav·a·gance**   *n*. a spending of more than is reasonable or necessary
17. **ex·trav·a·gant**   *adj*. 1. going beyond reasonable limits; excessive   2. costing or spending too much   —**ex·trav·a·gant·ly** *adv*.
18. **in·com·mu·ni·ca·ble**   *adj*. that cannot be communicated or told —**in·com·mu·ni·ca·bil·i·ty** *n*   —**in·com·mu·ni·ca·bly** *adv*.
19. **in·con·spic·u·ous**   *adj*. not conspicuous; attracting little attention —**in·con·spic·u·ous·ly** *adv*.   —**in·con·spic·u·ous·ness** *n*
20. **in·el·e·gant**   *adj*. not elegant; lacking refinement, good taste, grace, etc.; coarse, crude [*inelegant* manners]   —**in·el·e·gant·ly** *adv*.
21. **in·el·i·gi·ble**   *adj*. not eligible; not qualified under the rules [*ineligible* to vote] –*n*. an ineligible person   —**in·el·i·gi·bil·i·ty** *n*   —**in·el·i·gi·bly** *adv*.
22. **in·no·cence**   *n*. 1. freedom from sin or guilt   2. simplicity
23. **in·no·cent**   *n*. free from sin, evil or guilt   —**in·no·cent·ly** *adv*.
24. **in·tel·li·gence**   *n*. the ability to comprehend; to understand and profit from experience
25. **in·tel·li·gent**   *adj*. having or showing an alert mind or high intelligence; bright; clever, wise, etc.   —**in·tel·li·gent·ly** *adv*.
26. **in·sig·nif·i·cant**   *adj*. 1. having little or no importance or meaning; trivial [insignificant details]   2. small in size, amount, scope, etc. [to add an insignificant amount of salt] —**in·sig·nif·i·cance, in·sig·nif·i·can·cy** *n*   —**in·sig·nif·i·cant·ly** *adv*.
27. **mag·ni·fi·cence**   *n*. the quality of being magnificent, splendid, or grand
28. **mag·ni·fi·cent**   *adj*. beautiful in a grand or stately way; rich or splendid —**mag·ni·fi·cent·ly** *adv*.
29. **nav·i·ga·ble**   *adj*. 1. wide, deep, or free enough for ships, etc. to go through [a *navigable* river]   2. that can be steered or directed [a *navigable* balloon]

30. **nav·i·ga·tion**   *n.* 1. the science of locating the position and plotting the course of ships 2. the guidance of a ship or airplane   **—nav·i·ga·tion·al** *adj.*

31. **neg·li·gence**   *n.* the habitual failure to give proper care; laxity; inattentiveness

32. **neg·li·gent**   *adj.* 1. habitually failing to do the required thing 2. careless; lax; inattentive   **—neg·li·gent·ly** *adv.*

33. **out·ra·geous**   *adj.* so wrong or uncontrolled as to be shocking [to charge *outrageous* prices]   **—out·ra·geous·ly** *adv.*

34. **re·place**   *v.* **–placed, –plac·ing** 1. to put back in a former or proper position [*replace* the tools] 2. to take the place of [workers *replaced* by automated equipment]   **—re·place·a·ble** *adj.*   **—re·place·ment** *n.*

35. **re·place·a·ble**   *adj.* subject to being replaced

36. **re·place·ment**   *n.* a person or thing that takes the place of another that is lost, worn out, dismissed, etc.

37. **sig·nif·i·cance**   *n.* 1. meaning [the *significance* of the remark] 2. importance; consequence [a battle of great *significance*]

38. **sig·nif·i·cant**   *adj.* 1. full of meaning [a *significant* speech] 2. important; momentous [a *significant* occasion]   **—sig·nif·i·cant·ly** *adv.*

39. **sus·pi·cion**   *n.* the act of suspecting guilt, a wrong, etc. with little or no evidence

40. **sus·pi·cious**   *adj.* 1. causing or likely to cause suspicion [suspicious behavior] 2. tending to suspect evil, etc.   **—sus·pi·cious·ly** *adv.*

41. **un·am·big·u·ous**   *adj.* not indefinite or vague

42. **un·en·force·a·ble**   *adj.* 1. not able to be imposed by force 2. not able to force observance of (a law, etc.)

43. **un·in·tel·li·gent**   *adj.* 1. not having or using intelligence 2. not having or showing an alert mind or high intelligence; not bright, clever

44. **un·nav·i·ga·ble**   *adj.* 1. not wide or deep enough, or free enough from obstructions, for ships, etc. to go through 2. not able to be steered or directed

45. **un·sus·pi·cious**   *adj.* 1. not causing or likely to cause suspicion 2. not showing suspicion 3. not tending habitually to suspect evil, etc.

46. **venge·ance**   *n.* the return of an injury for an injury, in punishment; revenge

47. **venge·ful**   *adj.* seeking or wanting revenge

Practicing the words
A. Find the missing vowels for each word. Write the word and the abbreviation for its part of speech.

c_mm_n_c_bl_ ——————— — _nf_rc_ _bl_ ——————— —

_ _tr_g_ _ _s ——————— — s_gn_f_c_nc_ ——————— —

c_nv_nc_bl_ ——————— — m_gn_f_c_nt ——————— —

_l_g_nt ——————— — _xtr_v_g_nc_ ——————— —

_nn_c_nt ——————— — r_pl_c_ _bl_ ——————— —

n_v_g_bl_ ——————— — c_nsp_c_ _ _s ——————— —

c_nt_g_ _ _s ——————— — _nt_ll_g_nt ——————— —

_ppl_c_nt ——————— — s_sp_c_ _ _s ——————— —

_l_g_bl_ ——————— — _mb_g_ _ _s ——————— —

v_ng_ _nc_ ——————— — n_gl_g_nc_ ——————— —

B. Complete each sentence with a spelling word.

1. Even the huge ship was barely _____ during the storm.

2. Sarah groaned when she learned that the broken china was not _____.

3. What is the _____ of the fifty stars in the American flag?

4. Are porpoises more or less _____ than dogs?

5. His bright red beard made the celebrity _____ in a crowd.

6. Ruth felt that hiring a band was an unnecessary _____.

7. The police believe the new traffic law will be easily _____.

8. Due to your _____ none of the supplies will arrive on time.

9. Each _____ for the job must submit a sample of his or her writing.

10. The directions he gave us were _____ and confusing.

11. Is your skhtickl torah _____ to be printed in this zman's kovetz?

12. We had a _____ view of the mountains from our room.

13. In American courts, a jury will decide the guilt or _____ of the prisoner.

14. Shana's idea is so wild and _____ that it just might work!

C. Proofreading

Read the descriptions of the following titles. Cross out the nine misspelled words and write them correctly.

1. BORUCH'S ROPE

A sea captain promises vengeance when his magnificant, irreplaceable sailor's knot is untied by a suspicieous stranger.

2. DAYS OF OUR BRIBES

An eligable candidate for a veterinary degree must have a believable story as she protests her inocence of the charge of bribing sick dogs with milk bones.

3. ANOTHER CURL

The tragic, riches-to-rags story of elegent Ginger, who wastes her wealth on numerous outragious wigs.

4. ONE DATE AT A TIME

Yirmiyahu's feelings are ambigeous when he learns that his sore throat is neither contageous nor comunicable, but can be cured only by eating dried fruit.

1. _____   6. _____

2. _____   7. _____

3. _____   8. _____

4. _____   9. _____

5. _____

D. Follow each direction to make new forms of spelling words. Each direction can only be applied to the number of words for which there are spaces. For the last two, also use one of the new words. Use the spelling dictionary to help you.

1. Change **ence** to **ent** and add **ly**: _____ _____

2. Change **ance** to **ant** and add **ly**: _____ _____

3. Change **ious** to **ion**: _____ _____

4. Change **able** to **ment**: _____ _____

5. Change **able** to **ation**: _____ _____

6. Change **ance** to **ful**: _____

7. Add the negative prefix **un**: _____ _____

    _____ _____ _____

8. Add the negative prefix **in**: _____ _____

    _____ _____ _____

E. Fill in the blanks with the appropriate spelling word.

1. Some סופרים write very __ __ __ __ __ __ __ tefillin and mezuzos.

2. For some people it is an __ __ __ __ __ __ __ __ __ __ __ __ to eat שמורה מצה all 8 days of Pesach .

3. The מסילת ישרים compares עולם הזה to a __ __ __ __ __ __ __ __ __ maze – IF you get the right instructions.

4. The יצר הרע makes our way __ __ __ __ __ __ __ __ __ – blurring right and wrong.

5. Even __ __ __ __ __ __ __ __ __ __ people make mistakes.

6. A שומר חנם is responsible for __ __ __ __ __ __ __ __ __ __ – פשיעה.

7. Achashveirosh commanded that every __ __ __ __ __ __ __ __ maiden be brought to him.

8. Unlike allergies, the flu is __ __ __ __ __ __ __ __ __ __, so avoid spreading germs.

9. The __ __ __ __ __ __ __ __ __ __ claims by silly Democrats make me feel uncomfortable.

10. It is forbidden to take __ __ __ __ __ __ __ __ __ – it transgresses לא תקום.

11. Each __ __ __ __ __ __ __ __ __ hopes he gets accepted to camp.

12. It is of little __ __ __ __ __ __ __ __ __ __ __ whether you use a suitcase or duffel bag.

13. His feelings were barely __ __ __ __ __ __ __ __ __ __ __ because the words wouldn't come out.

14. The large letters were __ __ __ __ __ __ __ __ __ __ __, catching all eyes right away.

15. Our school is a __ __ __ __ __ __ __ __ __ __ educational organization.

16. __ __ __ __ __ __ __ __ __ is presumed until proven otherwise.

17. The rabble is easily __ __ __ __ __ __ __ __ __ __ by the fake news media.

18. The __ __ __ __ __ __ __ __ __ __ activity provoked investigation.

19. The תקנות of חז"ל are __ __ __ __ __ __ __ __ __ __ __ __ by חרם or מכת מרדות.

20. Money is __ __ __ __ __ __ __ __ __ __ __, but hurt emotions are difficult to repair.

189

Key Concepts
- assimilated prefixes
- padded sentences
- synonym
- connotation

We already learned that prefixes sometimes **assimilate**, or change to the following letter to accommodate easier pronunciation. Some prefixes always "assimilate" to **m** before the letters **b**, **m**, and **p** because it is easier to pronounce that way. The prefixes **con** and **in** both follow this pattern. They become **com** and **im** when joined to a root or base that begins with **b**, **m**, or **p**. They are spelled this way to make more compatible combinations that are easier to pronounce.

Say **in̲mediately** and **im̲mediately**. Say **con̲mute** and **com̲mute**.

This can sometimes cause a problem with tricky double consonants because one is from the prefix and one is from the root. Remembering that the prefix assimilated can help you remember to double the consonants.

A **padded sentence** has useless words or phrases. Even though it might seem to you that your writing sounds elegant, sophisticated, and elaborate because of all the extra words, it is really unnecessary to stuff your writing with extra fluff. Omit unnecessary words. The main idea should not be blurred by needless wordiness.

Synonyms are words that have similar meanings. The dictionary sometimes lists synonyms after the entry in a synonymy and explains some differences between the similar words. The exact meaning of a words is its denotation. On the other hand, a shade in meaning that is not the precise meaning of the word is its **connotation**. [In yeshivishe jargon, a connotation is the משמעות of the word.]

Lesson Spelling Rule: The prefixes **con** and **in** follow the same spelling pattern. Both are spelled with an **n** before most letters of the alphabet. Both are spelled with an **m** before roots or words that begin with the letters **b**, **m**, or **p**. Don't forget to double the consonants.

Mnemonic device: Remember co**mm**on co**mp**atible co**mb**inations.

1	CON +	GRESSIONAL = CONGRESSIONAL	11	IN +	TUITION = INTUITION
2	CON +	SERVATIVE = CONSERVATIVE	12	IN +	SULATION = INSULATION
3	CON +	NOTATION = CONNOTATION	13	IN +	NOCENT = INNOCENT
4	CON +	MENTATOR = COMMENTATOR	14	IN +	MUNITY = IMMUNITY
5	CON +	MUTE = COMMUTE	15	IN +	MORTALITY = IMMORTALITY
6	CON +	MERCIAL = COMMERCIAL	16	IN +	MEDIATELY = IMMEDIATELY
7	CON +	PETITION = COMPETITION	17	IN +	PATIENT = IMPATIENT
8	CON +	PUTER = COMPUTER	18	IN +	POSTOR = IMPOSTOR
9	CON +	PROMISE = COMPROMISE	19	IN +	PEACHED = IMPEACHED
10	CON +	BUSTION = COMBUSTION	20	IN +	BEDDED = IMBEDDED

A prefix may be spelled in several different ways.
Pay attention to the spelling words.

1. Look at the first three words in each column. Are the prefixes **con** and **in** spelled

   with an **n** or an **m** when they are added to form these words? _____

2. Why do the words **connotation** and **innocent** have double consonants?_____

   _____

3. Look at the remaining words in each column. How is the prefix **con** spelled when

   it is added to roots that begin with **b**, **m**, or **p**? _____

4. How is the prefix in spelled when it is added to words or roots that begin with **b**,

   m, or **p**? _____

The prefixes **con** and **in** become **com** and **im** when joined to a root or base that begins with **b**, **m**, or **p** to become easier to pronounce.
This sometimes causes a double consonant – remember that one is from the prefix and the other from the base.

Spelling Dictionary

1. **char·la·tan**   *n.* one who pretends to have expert knowledge or skill that he does not

2. **com·bus·tion**   *n.* 1. the act or process of burning   2. rapid oxidation accompanied by heat and, usually, light   —**com·bus·tive** *adj.*

3. **com·men·ta·tor**   *n.* 1, a person who gives (a series of remarks or observations)   2. a person who reports and analyzes news, sports, etc. as on radio or TV

4. **com·merce**   *n.* transactions

5. **com·mer·cial**   *adj.* of or connected with commerce or trade   *—n.* (*Radio & TV*) a paid advertisement   —**com·mer·cial·ly** *adv.*

6. **com·mute**   *v.* –**mut·ed, –mut·ing** 1. to change (an obligation, punishment, etc.) to one that is less severe   2. to travel as a commuter, a person who travels regularly between two points at some distance   —**com·mut·a·ble** *adj.*

7. **com·pe·ti·tion**   *n.* 1. a competing; rivalry   2. a contest, or match

8. **com·pro·mise**   *n.* a settlement in which each side gives up part of what it wants   — *v.* –**mised, –mis·ing** to settle by a compromise

9. **com·put·er**   *n.* an electronic machine used as a calculator or to store data

10. **con·gress**   *n.* 1. the social act of assembling for some common purpose   2. a meeting of elected or appointed represenetatives

11. **con·gres·sion·al**   *adj.* of a congress   —**con·gres·sion·al·ly** *adv.*

12. **con·no·ta·tion**   *n.* any idea suggested by or associated with a word, phrase, etc. in addition to its basic or literal meaning

13. **con·ser·va·tion**   *n.* 1. a protection from loss, waste, etc.   2. the official care and protection of natural resources, as forests   —**con·ser·va·tion·ist** *n.*

14. **con·ser·va·tive**   *adj.* tending to uphold established instituitions or methods and to resist or oppose any changes in these [*conservative* politics]   *–n.* a conservative person   —**con·ser·va·tive·ly** *adv.*

15. **con·serve**   *v.* –**served, –serv·ing** 1. keep in safety; protect from harm, loss, or destruction   2. use cautiously and frugally

16. **de·po·sit**   *v.* –**sit·ed, –sit·ing** to place or entrust, as for safekeeping   — *n.* 1. something placed for safekeeping; specif. money in a bank   2. a pledge or part payment

17. **ea·ger**   *adj.* impatient or anxious to do or get

18. **fidg·et·y**   *adj.* nervous, uneasy

19. **fraud**   *n.* a person who is not what he pretends to be

20. **fret·ful**   *adj.* irritated, worried

21. **im·bed**   *v.* –**bed·ded, –bed·ding** 1. to set or fix firmly in a surrounding mass [to imbed tiles in cement]   2. to fix in the mind

22. **im·me·di·ate·ly**   *adv.* without delay; at once [go home *immediately*]

23. **im·mor·tal**   *adj.* 1. not mortal; living or lasting forever   2. having lasting fame [an *immortal* poet]   —**im·mor·tal·i·ty** *n.*   —**im·mor·tal·ly** *adv.*

24. **im·mor·tal·i·ty**   *n.* the quality of being immortal

25. **im·mu·ni·ty**   *n., pl.* –**ties** resistance to or protection from disease

26. **im·pa·tient**   *adj.* feeling or showing restless eagerness or annoyanc because of delay, opposition, etc.

27. **im·peach**   *v.* --**peached, –peach·ing** to challenge the practices or honesty of; esp. to bring (a public official) to trial on a charge or wrongdoing

28. **im·pet·u·ous**   *adj.* acting with little thought

29. **im·pose**   *v.* **–posed, –pos·ing** 1. compel to behave a certain way   2. inflict something unpleasant

30. **im·po·si·tion**   *n.* a taking advantage of friendship, courtesy, etc. [staying for a meal when you are not invited is an *imposition*]

31. **im·pos·tor**   *n.* a person who cheats or deceives others, esp. by pretending to be someone or something that he or she is not

32. **in·no·cent**   *n.* free from sin, evil or guilt   **—in·no·cent·ly** *adv.*

33. **in·su·late**   *v.* **–lat·ed, –lat·ing** 1. place or set apart   2. protect from heat, cold, or noise by surrounding with insulating material

34. **in·su·la·tion**   *n.* any material used to insulate, to prevent the passage or leakage of electricity, heat, sound, etc.

35. **in·tu·i·tion**   *n.* the direct knowing or learning of something without conscious use of reasoning; instant understanding [to sense danger by a flash of *intuition*]

36. **men·tion**   *n.* 1. a remark that calls attention   2. official recognition of merit   *–v.* **–tioned, –tion·ing** 1. make reference to   2.commend

37. **mi·mic**   *n.* a person or thing that imitates

38. **mor·tal**   *adj.* 1. one that must eventually die [all *mortal* beings]   2. causing death; fatal [a *mortal* wound]   **—mor·tal·ly** *adv.*

39. **mor·tal·i·ty**   *n.* the condition of being mortal or sure to die

40. **no·ta·tion**   *n.* a written record of something

41. **op·pose**   *v.* **–posed, –pos·ing** 1. fight against; resist strongly   2. set against

42. **op·po·si·tion**   *n.* 1. resistance or struggle against [his plan met *opposition*]   2. anything that opposes

43. **pre·ser·va·tion**   *n.* 1. the activity of protecting something from loss or danger; saving   2. a process that saves organic matter from decay

44. **pre·serve**   *n.* a place where game, fish, etc. are protected or kept for controlled hunting and fishing   *–v.* **–served, –serv·ing** 1. protect, save [preserve our natural forests]   2. prepare (food), as by canning, salting, etc. for future use

45. [40]**quack**[1]   *n.* the noise made by a duck

46. **quack**[2]   *n.* a person without proper training who pretends to be a doctor

47. **res·er·va·tion**   *n.* a reserving or the thing reserved; specifi., *a)* public land set aside for special use [an Indian *reservation*] *b)* an arrangement by which a hotel room theater ticket, etc. is set aside for use at a certain time

48. **re·serve**   *n.* 1. formality and propriety of manner [behaved with *reserve*]   2. something kept back or saved for future use [crude oil *reserves*]   3. armed forces that are not on active duty but can be called on in an emergency   *–v.* 1. hold back or set

---

40 Words that have entirely different meanings, but are still spelled the same are called homographs. The dictionary lists them as separate entries, and differentiates between them with a small elevated number immediately after the entry word (superscript).

aside, esp. for future use [*reserve* the extra broth]   2. give or assign a resource for a particular person or cause [*reserve* me a seat]   3. arrange in advance [*reserve* a flight]

49.**serve**   *v.* 1. fulfill a function; perform a role [serves as secretary]   2. help with food or drink   3. put the ball into play

50.**ser·vice**   *n.* 1. work done or duty performed for others [repair *service*]   2. a religious ceremony [*services* begin at 8:00]   –*v.* –**viced, –vic·ing** 1. to furnish with a service   2. to make or keep fit for service, as by adjusting, repairing, etc. [we *service* kosher phones]

51.**tu·i·tion**   *n.* 1. teaching pupils individually   2. a fee paid for instruction

Practicing the words

A. First find and circle a form of the prefix **com** or **in** which is not scrambled. Then unscramble the rest of the letters to correctly spell one of the spelling words and write it on the line. Then mark which part of speech it is with the abbreviation.

1. sporimot   _____

2. upcomret   _____

3. comumet   _____

4. niotintiu   _____

5. subcomnoti   _____

6. nnoincet   _____

7. verseconivat   _____

8. dddeimbe   _____

9. lateiymedim   _____

10. cheapimde   _____

11. camecomril   _____

12. semporcomi   _____

13. talusinino   _____

14. saloniconserg   _____

15. nutimimy   _____

16. notitepicom   _____

17. tapimniet   _____

18. ononconitat   _____

19. taromimlyit   _____

20. tentramcomo   _____

195

B. Proofreading

A **padded sentence** has useless words and phrases. The main idea is buried by unnecessary words. A sentence can be improved by eliminating the unnecessary words.

~~What I think is that~~ houses should have proper insulation.
~~The reason why~~ I can't attend ~~is~~ because I have to babysit that night.
~~What~~ Carol wants ~~is for~~ you to write the song.

Cross out the unnecessary words in each padded sentence. Then rewrite it on your looseleaf paper by omitting the unnecessary words.

1. What I mean is that the computer is a valuable machine.

_____

2. Carlo will be the commentator and the reason is because he is a clever speaker.

_____

3. War was avoided because of the fact that both countries agreed to compromise.

_____

4. What I think is that the senator should not be impeached.

_____

5. The thing is, this vaccine provides immunity from polio.

_____

6. What I went to the doctor for was to have this imbedded splinter removed.

_____

7. The reason why Leah seems impatient is because she is nervous.

_____

C. Find and write the spelling word that is either a synonym or antonym for each word. Then write A or S to show if the spelling word is a synonym or antonym. Then write the abbreviation for the part of speech.

1. contest _____ ___ _____

2. liberal _____ ___ _____

3. unhurried _____ ___ _____

4. later _____ ___ _____

5. advertisement _____ ___ _____

6. fire _____ ___ _____

7. accused _____ ___ _____

8. eternity _____ ___ _____

9. insight _____ ___ _____

10. faker _____ ___ _____

11. guilty _____ ___ _____

12. resistance _____ ___ _____

D. Connotations

A connotation is a special shade of meaning associated with a word. Both skinny and slender mean "thin," but slender has a more complimentary connotation. Skinny is less respectable.

The words spreading out from the spelling word are synonyms for the spelling word at the base. They have the same general meaning, but different connotations or shades of meaning. Choose the synonym with the *best* connotation for each sentence. Carefully read the definition in your spelling dictionary for each word. The underlined word in each sentence is an association clue. Paying attention to the underlined word will assist you in choosing the best match.

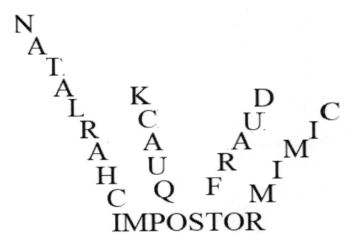

IMPOSTOR

1. The man <u>posing</u> as the king was a(n) _____.

2. The _____ claimed that his medicine <u>cured</u> everything.

3. The audience actually believed that the _____ was an <u>expert</u> on UFO's.

4. The _____ did an amazing <u>imitation</u> of the president.

5. After <u>cheating</u> people out of their money, the _____ left town.

198

E. Do the same thing for this spelling word. The underlined words serve as clues to help you with the distinctions.

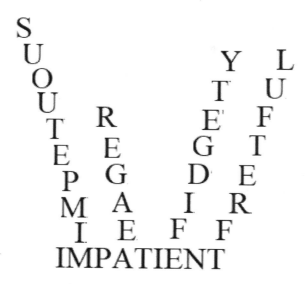

1. Benjy was _____ to leave for an <u>exciting</u> trip over the off-Shabbos.

2. The _____ child <u>burst into</u> the room without knocking.

3. <u>As soon as</u> the light turned green, the _____ driver blew his horn.

4. The _____ baby <u>cried</u> for its bottle.

5. The _____ diner <u>toyed with</u> the fork and <u>twisted</u> the napkin into knots.

F. Build a word pyramid by following the code. Use your spelling dictionary to find the four pyramid words that match the definitions.

The root **pos** means "to put or position."

1. one who put himself in another's place

_____

2. those who take the opposite position in an argument

_____

3. an idea put before others

_____

4. something that puts a burden on a person

_____

		P	O	S						
		P	O	S	11	12	10	3		
	4	6	P	O	S	11	8	10		
	2	3	P	O	S	4	11			
9	10	8	P	O	S	1	5			
	8	9	P	O	S	4	11	4	8	7
	4	6	P	O	S	4	11	4	8	7

A	D	E	I	L	M	N	O	P	R	T	U
1	2	3	4	5	6	7	8	9	10	11	12

Build another pyramid. Find the four pyramid words that match the definitions.

The word **serv** means "to help, keep."

1. one who keeps to established methods

_____

2. a program to keep natural resources safe

_____

3. that which can still help or be of use

_____

4. to keep safe or protected

_____

		S	E	R	V					
		S	E	R	V	5	3	4		
9	10	4	S	E	R	V	4			
	10	4	S	E	R	V	1	11	5	8	7
3	8	7	S	E	R	V	1	11	5	12	4
		S	E	R	V	5	3	4	1	2	6
3	8	7	S	E	R	V	1	11	5	8	7

A	B	C	E	I	L	N	O	P	R	T
1	2	3	4	5	6	7	8	9	10	1

G. Fill in the blanks with the appropriate spelling words.

1. Silly Democrats __ __ __ __ __ __ __ __ President Trump - twice.

2. Make sure the tick's proboscis does not remain __ __ __ __ __ __ __ __ in the skin.

3. A __ __ __ __ __ __ __ __ __ __ __ Democrat is scarce.

4. A __ __ __ __ __ __ __ __ __ __ __ is a special shade of meaning associated with a word.

5. Most bochurim will not listen to a news __ __ __ __ __ __ __ __ __ __ .

6. Most of you __ __ __ __ __ __ __ to and from school on the bus.

7. The billboard shows __ __ __ __ __ __ __ __ __ __ announcements – a.k.a. advertisements.

8. The two parties made a __ __ __ __ __ __ __ __ __ __ to prevent a silly war.

9. The פורים שטיק created a __ __ __ __ __ __ __ __ __ __ __ in the בית מדרש.

10. צדיקים have great __ __ __ __ __ __ __ __ because they are close to Hashem.

11. The oldest __ __ __ __ __ __ __ __ __ __ __ __ committee is the Ways and Means committee.

12. The sturdy __ __ __ __ __ __ __ __ __ __ kept the temperature from changing too drastically.

13. The impeached official was found to be __ __ __ __ __ __ __ __ and was

acquitted.

14. It took a long time to attain herd __ __ __ __ __ __ __ __ from COVID.

15. אמונה in the __ __ __ __ __ __ __ __ __ __ of our נפש is a basic

requirement.

16. מצוות should be performed __ __ __ __ __ __ __ __ __ __ __, without

delay.

17. I am __ __ __ __ __ __ __ __ __ for summer vacation to arrive.

18. שבתי צבי ימ"ש was an __ __ __ __ __ __ __ __, a false משיח.

19. There was class __ __ __ __ __ __ __ __ __ __ to write the best essay.

20. Having an unfiltered __ __ __ __ __ __ __ __ can be risky to your נשמה.

Key Concepts

- assimilated prefixes

Some more common prefixes and their assimilations. If they were always added directly to the base or root, some consonant combinations would be difficult to pronounce.

For example: a<u>d</u>ford di<u>s</u>ficult su<u>b</u>focate co<u>n</u>respond co<u>n</u>lapse

Instead, afford, difficult, suffocate, correspond, collapse.

They assimilate for purposes of easier pronunciation, but complicate the spelling because of the unexpected double consonants. It helps if you can remember the prefix and how it assimilated.

Lesson Spelling Rule: Assimilated prefixes solve pronunciation problems but cause spelling problems. Double consonants result when the last letter of the prefix changes to match the first letter of the root.

Prefixes used in this lesson:

- ad- motion towards; addition to; nearness to
- dis- away, apart; not; opposite of
- sub- under, beneath; lower in rank or position; to a lesser degree than; by or forming a division into smaller parts
- ob- to, toward, before; opposed to, against; completely, totally
- con- with or together; very or very much; all together
- in- no, not, without; in, into, within, on, toward

1	AD +	FORD	= AFFORD	11 COM+ RESPONDENT	= CORRESPONDENT
2	AD +	FLICTION	= AFFLICTION	12 COM+ RUPT	= CORRUPT
3	AD +	FIRMATIVE	= AFFIRMATIVE	13 IN + RESPONSIBLE	= IRRESPONSIBLE
4	AD +	FECTION	= AFFECTION	14 IN + RIGATION	= IRRIGATION
5	DIS +	FICULT	= DIFFICULT	15 IN + RESISTIBLE	= IRRESISTIBLE
6	SUB +	FERED	= SUFFERED	16 COM+ LISION	= COLLISION
7	SUB +	FOCATE	= SUFFOCATE	17 COM+ LAPSE	= COLLAPSE
8	SUB +	FICIENT	= SUFFICIENT	18 IN + LUMINATE	= ILLUMINATE
9	OB +	FICIAL	= OFFICIAL	19 IN + LEGIBLE	= ILLEGIBLE
10	OB +	FERED	= OFFERED	20 IN + LITERATE	= ILLITERATE

Pay attention to the spelling words.

1. When the prefixes in the first column are joined to roots that being with the letter **f**, how does the spelling of each prefix change? _____ becomes _____, _____ becomes _____, _____ becomes _____, and _____ becomes _____.

2. The roots in the second column begin with the letter **r** or **l**. When the prefixes **con** and **in** are joined to the letter **r**, **con** is spelled _____, and **in** is spelled _____.

3. When **con** and **in** are joined to the letter **l**, **con** is spelled _____, and **in** is spelled _____.

4. In all of the prefixes, which letter changes to match the first letter of the root? _____

5. What common spelling problem might occur in all of the list words because the prefixes are assimilated into the roots? _____

> Assimilated prefixes solve pronunciation problems but cause spelling problems. Double consonants result when the last letter of the prefix changes to match the first letter of the root.

Spelling Dictionary

1. **af·fec·tion**   *n.* fond or tender feeling

2. **af·firm·a·tive**   *adj.* answering "yes" [an *affirmative* reply]   *—n.* a word or expression indicating agreement   **—af·firm·a·tive·ly** *adv.*

3. **af·flic·tion**   *n.* anything causing pain or distress

4. **af·ford**   *v.* to have enough or the means for; bear the cost of

5. **as·sis·tant**   *adj.* assisting; helping [the store's *assistant* manager]   *—n.* a person who assists another or serves in a lower position; helper

6. **col·lapse**   *v.* **–lapsed, –lap·sing** 1. to fall down or cave in   2. to break down suddenly in health   *—n.* a failure or breakdown, as in business, health, etc.

7. **col·lide**   *v.* **–lid·ed, –lid·ing** to come into conflict; to crash together with violent impact

8. **col·li·sion**   *n.* a colliding, or coming together with sudden, violent force

9. **con·sis·ten·cy** *n., pl.* **–cies** 1. firmness or thickness, as of a liquid   2. a being consistent in practice or principle [he is unpredictable because he lacks *consistency*]

10. **con·sis·tent**   *adj.* 1. the same throughout in structure and composition   2. in agreement; in harmony [the testimony was *consistent* with the facts]

11. **cor·res·pon·dent**   *n.* a person hired by a newspaper to send news regularly from a distant city or country

12. **cor·rupt**   *adj.* changed from good to bad; having become dishonest [accepting bribes made him a *corrupt* official]   *–v.* to make or become corrupt   **— cor·rupt·ness** *n.*

13. **de·sist**   *v.* **–sis·ted, –sis·ting** to stop doing something

14. **des·pon·dent**   *adj.* dejected, discouraged [he was *despondent* over the loss of his job]

15. **dif·fi·cult**   *adj.* 1. hard to do, make, understand, etc.   2. hard to satisfy, persuade, etc. [he was a *difficult* employer]

16. **il·leg·i·ble**   *adj.* difficult or impossible to read because badly written or printed, faded, etc.   **—il·leg·i·bil·i·ty** *n.*   **—il·leg·i·bly** *adv.*

17. **il·lit·er·ate**   *adj.* uneducated; esp., not knowing how to read or write   *—n.* an illiterate person; esp., one not knowing how to read or write

18. **il·lu·mi·nate**   *v.* **–nat·ed, –nat·ing** to give light to, to light up [candles *illuminated* the room]   **—il·lu·mi·na·tion** *n.*

19. **im·pos·si·ble**   *adj.* not possible; not capable of being or happening   **— im·pos·si·bly** *adv.*

20. **in·ac·ces·si·ble**   *adj.* 1. that cannot be seen, talked to, etc. [an *inaccessible* public official] 2. not obtainable   **—in·ac·ces·si·bly** *adv*

21. **in·cred·i·ble**   *adj.* 1. not credible; unbelievable [an incredible story]   2. so great, unusual, etc. as to seem impossible [incredible speed]   **—in·cred·i·bil·i·ty** *n.* **—in·cred·i·bly** *adv.*

22. **in·ed·i·ble**   *adj.* not fit to be eaten

23. **in·ex·press·ible**   *adj.* that cannot be expressed or described [*inexpressible* sorrow]

24. **in·tan·gi·ble**   *adj.* not tangible; specif., *a)* that cannot be touched *b)* not material or physical; abstract *c)* hard to define or understand clearly [an *intangible* feeling of dread]   **—in·tan·gi·bil·i·ty** *n.*   **—in·tan·gi·bly** *adv.*

25. **in·vin·ci·ble**   *adj.* that cannot be defeated or overcome; unconquerable   **—in·vin·ci·bil·i·ty** *n.* **—in·vin·ci·bly** *adv.*

26. **ir·re·sis·ti·ble**   *adj.* that cannot be resisted [an *irresistible* force]
    —**ir·re·sis·ti·bil·i·ty** *n.*   —**ir·re·sis·ti·bly** *adv.*
27. **ir·res·pon·si·ble**   *adj.* lacking a sense of responsibility; unreliable, lazy, etc.
    —**ir·res·pon·si·bil·i·ty** *n.*   —**ir·res·pon·si·bly** *adv.*
28. **ir·re·vers·i·ble**   *adj.* that cannot be undone or annulled [an *irreversible* decision]
29. **ir·ri·gate**   *v.* –**gat·ed,** –**gat·ing** to supply (land) with water   —
    ir·ri·ga·tion *n.*
30. **of·fer**   *v.* –**fered** or –**ferred,** –**fer·ing** or –**fer·ring** to present for acceptance or
    consideration [to *offer* one's services]
31. **of·fi·cial**   *adj.* by, from, or with the proper authority [an *official* request]   —*n.* a
    person holding office   —**of·fi·cial·ly** *adv.*
32. **re·sist**   *v.* –**sist·ed,** –**sist·ing** oppose or withstand; refuse to comply
33. **re·sis·ti·ble**   *adj.* capable of being resisted, withstood, or frustrated
34. **res·pon·si·ble**   *adj.* 1. being the agent or cause of   2. held accountable   3. worthy of
    having trust   —**res·pon·si·bil·i·ty** *n.*   —**res·pon·si·bly** *adv.*
35. **res·pon·si·bi·li·ty**   *n., pl.* –**ties** 1. the condition of being responsible [he accepted
    responsibility for the error]   2. a person or thing that one is responsible for [arranging flights is
    your *responsibility*]
36. **spon·sor**   *n.* 1. a person or agency that agrees toi be responsible for, advise, or
    support a person, group, or activity   2. a business firm or other agency that pays for a radio or
    TV program on which it advertises something   –*v.* –**sor·ed,** –**sor·ing** to act as a sponsor for
37. **suf·fered**   *v.* –**fered** or –**ferred ,** –**fer·ing** or –**fer·ring** to undergo pain, harm, loss,
    a penalty, etc. [she *suffered* in the heat]   —**suf·fer·ing** *n.*
38. **suf·fi·cient**   *adj.* as much as is needed; enough [*sufficient* supplies to last through the
    month]   —**suf·fi·cien·tly** *adv.*
39. **suf·fo·cate**   *v.* –**cat·ed,** –**cat·ing** to die by cutting off the supply of oxygen to the
    lungs, gills, etc.   —**suf·fo·cat·ing** *n.*

Practicing the words
A. Find the fiften spelling words hidden in three directions in the puzzle →↓↑ Write each word.

I	R	R	E	S	P	O	N	S	I	B	L	E	I
R	C	O	L	L	A	P	S	E	L	A	A	V	L
R	T	E	B	C	M	R	U	N	L	F	I	I	L
E	L	T	I	H	V	U	F	G	I	F	C	T	U
S	U	A	G	W	Z	S	F	O	T	E	I	A	M
I	C	C	E	M	J	K	E	Y	E	C	F	M	I
S	I	O	L	U	M	B	R	T	R	T	F	R	N
T	F	F	L	D	C	H	E	K	A	I	O	I	A
I	F	F	I	R	S	U	D	T	T	O	X	F	T
B	I	U	L	O	H	M	Y	B	E	N	D	F	E
L	D	S	U	F	F	I	C	I	E	N	T	A	O
E	O	F	F	E	R	E	D	A	F	F	O	R	D

1. _____
2. _____
3. _____
4. _____
5. _____
6. _____
7. _____
8. _____

9. _____
10. _____
11. _____
12. _____
13. _____
14. _____
15. _____

207

B.Find the misspelled word in each group and write the word correctly.

1. irrigation	2. suffocate	3.collapse
oficial	difficult	corupt
suffered	afliction	illuminate
correspondent	afford	suffocate

_____

4. colision	5. corrupted	6.correspondent
affliction	irigation	irresistible
illiterate	sufficient	illuminate
affection	offered	ilegible

_____

C. Rewrite each phrase by substituting a spelling word similar in meaning for each underlined word. Then expand each rewritten phrase into a sentence.

1. enough water _____ _____

_____

_____

2. underwent a breakdown _____ _____

_____

_____

3. presented sentiment _____ _____

_____

_____

4. unreliable reporter _____ _____

_____

_____

5. dishonest officeholder _____ _____

_____

_____

6. elighten the uneducated _____ _____

_____

_____

7. hard to buy _____ _____

_____

_____

8. alluring assent _____ _____

_____

_____

D. Add the suffix **ible** and the correct form of the negative prefix in to each word or root in the list below. Write each new word beside a synonym that is spelled with the **un** prefix and the **able** prefix. The first two words are on your spelling list.

    access reverse vinc express poss   ed   leg response cred tang

1. unreliable   _____

2. unreadable   _____

3. unbeatable   _____

4. unachievable   _____

5. unchewable   _____

6. unspeakable   _____

7. untouchable   _____

8. unbelievable   _____

9. unchangeable   _____

10. unattainable   _____

Mnemonic device: Think of the word **unable** to remind you that the prefix **un** and the suffix **able** frequently go together.

Now make up your own mnemonic device to help you remember that words that use a prefix beginning with the letter **i** often use a suffix that begins with the letter **i**.

_____

E. Build a word pyramid by following the code. Use your spelling dictionary to find the four pyramid words that match the definitions.

The root **spon** means "promise."

1. not doing what is promised

							S	P	O	N								
							S	P	O	N	11	9	10					
				10	5		S	P	O	N	11	6	13	5				
				4	5		S	P	O	N	4	5	8	12				
	6	10	10	5		S	P	O	N	11	6	2	7	5			
3	9	10	10	5		S	P	O	N	4	5	8	12				
			10	5		S	P	O	N	11	6	2	6	7	6	12	14	

B	C	D	E	I	L	N	O	R	S	T	V	Y
2	3	4	5	6	7	8	9	10	11	12	13	14

_____

2. one who promises to support or be responsible for another _____

3. a doing of what is promised

4. a feeling that there is no hope or promise

_____   _____

Build another pyramid. Find the four pyramid words that match the definitions.

The root **sist** means "to stand."

1. one who stands by to help

_____

2. continuing to "stand through," refusing to give up

_____

3. stood back fromm stopped doing

_____

4. can't be withstood

						S	I	S	T				
		6	8			S	I	S	T				
		4	5			S	I	S	T	5	4		
		1	12			S	I	S	T	1	8	13	
	10	5	11			S	I	S	T	5	8	13	
	3	9	8			S	I	S	T	5	8	3	14
6	11	11	5			S	I	S	T	6	2	7	5

A	B	C	D	E	I	L	N	O	P	R	S	T	Y
1	2	3	4	5	6	7	8	9	10	11	12	13	14

F. Fill in the blanks with the appropriate spelling word.

1. The economy's __ __ __ __ __ __ __ __ led to a terrible depression.

2. The U.S. claims to __ __ __ __ __ __ protection to people who suffer.

3. __ __ __ __ __ __ __ __ __ __ __ action means doing positively.

4. An __ __ __ __ __ __ __ __ __ __ person has not learned to read.

5. It is sometimes __ __ __ __ __ __ __ __ __ to come up with suitable sentences.

6. Yiddin are commanded to have __ __ __ __ __ __ __ __ __ for each other – ואהבת לרעך כמוך.

7. Some masks might cause one to __ __ __ __ __ __ __ __ and be uncomfortable.

8. Having disease is a great __ __ __ __ __ __ __ __ __ __.

9. The government __ __ __ __ __ __ __ __ refused to commit himself to provide assistance.

10. The invalid __ __ __ __ __ __ __ __ great pains.

11. Their news __ __ __ __ __ __ __ __ __ __ __ __ doesn't always state the entire truth.

12. The __ __ __ __ __ __ __ officials accepted bribes.

13. An __ __ __ __ __ __ __ __ __ __ __ __ __ government does not adequately support its military.

14. Class time is usually __ __ __ __ __ __ __ __ __ to complete the required work.

15. He was accustomed to the idea that his charm was __ __ __ __ __ __ __ __ __ __ __ __.

16. The driver avoided a __ __ __ __ __ __ __ __ __ by swiftly turning the wheel.

17. מצרים relied on the נילוס for __ __ __ __ __ __ __ __ __ __ of their fields.

18. Many people use a flashlight to __ __ __ __ __ __ __ __ __ the rooms during בדיקת חמץ.

19. Some students still turn in __ __ __ __ __ __ __ __ __ papers.

20. They __ __ __ __ __ __ __ him sufficient reasons.

212

Spelling Lesson 21

Key Concepts
- Quirky **q**

The letter **q** is always followed by the letter **u** in the English language. This is because on its own, the letter would be pronounced like **k**, as in Iraq. The u tells you to add either the sound of **w** and does not function as a vowel. To make it more confusing, there are some words in which the **qu** is still pronounced as **k**. As an extra confusing twist, at the end of a word it is always pronounced **k**, but it is even spelled with an extra (useless) silent vowel – **e**.

The pronunciation of **q** is usually **kw**, but never at the end of a word.
At the end of a word, it is always spelled **que** and always pronounced **k** (plaque).
At the beginning of a word it is always pronounced **kw** (quarrel).
In the middle of a word, it can be pronounced as **k** (conquer) or **kw** (equator).

In other words, at the end of a word, it is never pronounced **kw**. At the beginning of a word it is always pronounced **kw**.

Lesson Spelling Rule: The letter **q** is always followed by **u** in the English language, but is sometimes pronounced **k**, usually **kw**. At the end of a word (it is always pronounced **k** and) it is always spelled **que**.

1. UNI<u>QU</u>E   2. AC<u>QU</u>IRE   3. <u>QU</u>IZZICAL

4. CLI<u>QU</u>E   5. AC<u>QU</u>AINTED   6. <u>QU</u>IVER

7. PLA<u>QU</u>E   8. ADE<u>QU</u>ATELY   9. <u>QU</u>ESTIONNAIRE

                   10. COLLO<u>QU</u>IAL   11. <u>QU</u>ARANTINE

12. MAS<u>QU</u>ERADE   13. IN<u>QU</u>ISITIVE   14. <u>QU</u>ENCH

15. CON<u>QU</u>ER   16. BAN<u>QU</u>ET   17. <u>QU</u>AINT

18. LAC<u>QU</u>ER   19. SE<u>QU</u>EL   20. <u>QU</u>INTUPLET

Pay attention to the spelling words.

1. Look at the underlined letters in each word. What letter always follows the letter q? _____

2. Say the first three words to yourself. What two letters make the single sound of the letter k? ____

3. What silent letter follows these letters? ____

4. In the next three words in the first column, what two letters make the sound of k? ____

5. In the remaining words on the spelling list, what two letters make the sound of kw? ____

The letter **q** is always followed by **u** in the English language, but is sometimes pronounced **k**, usually **kw**. At the end of a word (it is always pronounced **k** and) it is always spelled **que**.

1. **ac·quaint**   *v.* **–quaint·ed, –quaint·ing** to make thouroughly familiar with

2. **ac·quire**   *v.* **–quired, –quir·ing** to come to have as one's own [to *acquire* knowledge]

3. **ac·qui·si·tion**   *n.* something acquired

4. **ad·e·quate**   *adj.* 1. enough or good enough; sufficient   2. barely satisfactory   **—ad·e·quate·ly** *adv.*

5. **ban·quet**   *n.* an elaborate meal; feast

6. **clique**   *n.* a small, exclusive circle of people

7. **col·lo·qui·al**   *adj.* being or containing the words, phrases, and idioms that are commonly used in informal speech and writing; informal   **—col·lo·qui·al·ly** *adv.*

8. **con·quer**   *v.* **–quered, –quer·ing** to overcome by physical, mental, or moral force; defeat   **—con·quer·or** *n.*

9. **cri·tique**   *n.* a critical analysis or evaluation of a subject, situation, book, etc.   *–v.* **–qued** appraise critically

10. **e·qui·nox**   *n.* 1. the time when the sun crosses the equator, making night and day of equal length in all parts of the earth: the **vernal equinox** occurs about March 21, the **autumnal equinox** about September 22   2. either of the two points on the celestial equator where the sun crosses it on these dates

11. **gro·tesque**   *adj.* having a twisted, strange, unreal appearance, shape, etc.; bisarre   **—gro·tesque·ly** *adv.* **—gro·tesque·ness** *n.*

12. **in·qui·ry**   *n. pl.,* **–ries** 1. an investigation or examination   2. a question; query

13. **in·qui·si·tive**   *adj.* 1. inclined to ask many questions or seek information 2. asking more questions than is necessary or proper; prying   **—in·qui·si·tive·ly** *adv.*   **—in·qui·si·tive·ness** *n.*

14. **jon·quil**   *n.* a narcissus having relatively small yellow flowers and long, slender leaves

15. **lac·quer**   *n.* a resin varnish obtained from certain trees, used to give a hard, smooth, highly polished finish to wood   *–v.* **–quered, –quer·ing** to coat with or as with lacquer

16. **man·ne·quin**   *n.* a model of the human body, used by window dressers artists, etc.

17. **mas·quer·ade**   *n.* a ball or party at which masks and fancy costumes are worn   *–v.* **–ad·ed, –ad·ing** to take part in a masquerade

18. **pic·tur·esque**   *adj.* 1. having a wild or natural beauty, as mountain scenery 2. suggesting a mental picture; vivid [a *picturesque* description]

19. **plaque**   *n.* 1. any thin, flat piece of metal, wood, etc. used as a decoration or to commemorate or identify something   2. (pathology) a small abnormal patch on or in the body

20. **quaint**   *adj.* 1. unusual or old-fashioned in a pleasing way   2. unusual; curious; odd   **—quaint·ly** *adv.*   **—quaint·ness** *n.*

21. **quar·an·tine**   *n.* isolation or restriction on travel to keep contagious diseases, insect pests, etc. from spreading   *–v.* **–tined, –tin·ing** to place under quarantine

22. **quar·ry**   *n. pl.,* **–ries** a place where building stone, marble, or slate is excavated   *–v.* **–ried, –ry·ing** to excavate from a quarry

23. **quench**   *v.* **–quired, –quir·ing** 1. to extinguish, put out [water *quenched* the fire]   2. to satisfy; slake [he *quenched* his thirst]   — **quench·a·ble** *adj.*   **—quench·less** *adj.*

24. **ques·tion·naire**   *n.* a written or printed list of questions used in gathering information from one or more persons

25. **quin·tup·let**   *n.* 1. any of five offspring born at a single birth   2. a group of five, usually or one kind

26. **qui·ver**   *v.* **–vered, –ver·ing** to shake with a tremulous motion; tremble   **—qui·ver·y** *adj.*

27. **quiz·zi·cal**   *adj.* 1. gently mocking or teasing [a quizzical smile]   2. perplexed; questioning [a quizzical look on his face]   — **quiz·zi·cal·ly** *adv.*

28. **se·quel**   *n.* something that follows; continuation

29. **u·nique**   *adj.* having no like or equal; unparalleled   **—u·nique·ly** *adv.*   **—u·nique·ness** *n.*

Practicing the words

A. Write in alphabetical order the spelling words in which **qu** has the sound of **k** in the left column. Then write in alphabetial order the spelling words that begin with the sound of **kw** in the right column.

_____   _____

_____   _____

_____   _____

_____   _____

_____   _____

_____

B. The words in each group are related in some way. Find the spelling word that fits each group. Then indicate what part of speech it is.

1. twin   triplet   quadruplet   _____ _____

2. sole   exclusive   only   _____ _____

3. get   obtain   procure   _____ _____

4. sufficiently suitable   satisfactorily _____ _____

5. shake   tremble   shiver   _____ _____

6. idiomatic   slang   informal   _____ _____

7. feast   dinner   meal   _____ _____

8. party   festival   gala   _____ _____

9. group   association   club   _____ _____

10. strange   unusual   eccentric   _____ _____

11. defeat   overcome   subdue   _____ _____

12. curious   quizzical   prying   _____ _____

13. extinguish   satisfy   appease   _____ _____

14. detention   isolation   restriction   _____ _____

15. continuation follow-up   installment   _____ _____

C. Complete this story with spelling words.

Moishy adjusted his costume as he arrived at the Purim __1__ party. He began to __2__ with excitement. He was well __3__ with everyone, but he couldn't recognize anyone. One person had measle spots painted on his face. A sign around his neck said, "Don't talk to me: I'm in __4__." Moishy saw an Egyptian king who had Paraoh II painted on his cloak. Behind him walked Paraoh III, his __5__. Moishy edged closer to the long __6__ table, which was covered with food. He helped himself to a glass of lemonade to __7__ his thirst. As he looked around, he saw no one else dressed like him and was certain that his costume was __8__. It might even win the __9__ that was being awarded as first prize. Just then he glanced at tho door. There he saw not two, not three, but four other people dressed as the same Rubik's Cube. Instead of being original, he was one in five. Maybe he could say that he had come as a __10__.

1. _____   6. _____

2. _____   7. _____

3. _____   8. _____

4. _____   9. _____

5. _____   10. _____

D. Find nine new **que/qu** words. Begin with the word **quiz** and find your way out of the

maze. Write each new word.

quiz

1. _____

2. _____

3. _____

4. _____

5. _____

6. _____

7. _____

8. _____

9. _____

L	Q	U	A	R	R	Y	
I	N	Q	U	I	R	Y	E	C
U	I	Q	U	E	G	R	O	U
Q	N	S	I	T	I	Q	T	I
N	I	E	R	Q→U	U	E	N
O	U	R	C	Z←I	E	S	C
J	Q	U	T	C	I	P	Q	X
N	E	N	N	A	M	E	U	A
O	I	T	I	S	I	U	Q	C

Unscramble the following sentences. Use one of your new words to complete each one.

You may add endings.

1. 21 is March the of date spring the _____ .

   _____

2. won grandmother prize her a for _____ .

   _____

3. is think I that odd statue _____ .

   _____

4. received play a the good _____ .

   _____

220

5. rock brother the works my at_____ .

_____

6. country drive a is the always in_____ .

_____

7. Mordechai a still stood as as_____ .

_____

8. when museum new exhibit will the its_____ .

_____

9. the your enclose receipt with _____ .

_____

E. Fill in the blanks with the appropriate spelling word.

1. פורים is really __ __ __ __ __ __ because there is a מצוה to drink much wine.

2. המן stood out from the rest of אחשורוש's __ __ __ __ __ __ __ of special advisors.

3. __ __ __ __ __ __ __ forms on teeth if you will not brush frequently.

4. Plenty of people will __ __ __ __ __ __ __ __ __ __ __ on פורים.

5. אחשורוש paid money so he did not need to __ __ __ __ __ __ __ in order to rule.

6. A shiny coating of __ __ __ __ __ __ __ helps the crumbs wash off the challah board.

7. המן offered money to __ __ __ __ __ __ __ the right to annihilate the אידין.

8. Over the vacation you might have become __ __ __ __ __ __ __ __ __ __ with some new friends.

9. I hope that you __ __ __ __ __ __ __ __ __ __ experienced the קדושה of יום טוב.

10. Slang is often used in __ __ __ __ __ __ __ __ __ correspondence.

11. We try to make children __ __ __ __ __ __ __ __ __ __ __ __ on the סדר night.

12. אחשורוש made a very long __ __ __ __ __ __ __ for 180 days.

13. The __ __ __ __ __ __ __ of the נס פורים was a second קבלת התורה באהבה.

14. אחשורוש likely wore a __ __ __ __ __ __ __ __ __ expression when he asked מי הוא זה ואי זה הוא?

15. A fancy word for a little shiver or tremble is __ __ __ __ __ __ __.

16. You often fill out a __ __ __ __ __ __ __ __ __ __ __ __ __ when submitting an application.

17. We were sick and tired of forced __ __ __ __ __ __ __ __ __ to try limiting

    COVID.

18. It is better to __ __ __ __ __ __ your thirst with water instead of soda.

19. On פסח many people still prepare food in __ __ __ __ __ __, old-fashioned ways.

20. A __ __ __ __ __ __ __ __ __ has 4 other siblings born with him.

Made in the USA
Columbia, SC
30 August 2024